Be Less

...At Sa

CONTENTS:

- Foreword

FOREWORD

"Hi, my name is David and I am shit".

Much has been written over the years about how to succeed, be the best, be number one, dominate, rule, conquer and more recently something called slay (?) but I have often thought that for lots of people, never mind being the best...there is probably a level of comfort in just being a bit less shit.

It doesn't matter what you do, the fact is that somebody is always going to be better than you, either now or eventually. Given the inevitability of this, doesn't it make more sense for mere mortals to set their sights on the warm and fuzzy prospect of just being a bit less shit? While the Highly Effective people and their Habits have their book, what if you are not Highly Effective and don't want to be? What happened to the "five rules of scraping by for lazy shitters"? Society today is supposed to be more inclusive than exclusive and I for one am not about to alienate the vast majority of the population who aren't even moderately effective, let along highly effective. Shitters, this one is for you.

With a (now largely irrelevant) university education in Law and French, I was relatively academic as a kid, but to the horror of my Northern working-class parents at the time, I did nothing with my law degree. As it happens, my lawyer friends now credit me for demonstrating incredible foresight at such a young age in giving the legal profession a wide berth. I only speak French if I am on holiday and need to order a meal or another beer. Oh yes, I speak it beautifully and sound like an educated native, but I have not really used it professionally. Looking back, I wonder if I had already quickly and perhaps semi-consciously come to terms with the idea that other students in my group were better than me and perhaps more focused than I was on their ultimate career goal. Or maybe I just felt more at home in the company of the slackers, chancers and opportunists, you know, your average shitters.

Don't get me wrong. I am not totally stupid. A 2:1 from a decent university in a rigorous academic discipline allowed me to return home having enjoyed my four years of higher education with a piece of paper that enabled my folks to tell their friends that their favourite (only) son had confounded expectations and turned out to be semi-intelligent life form. While they were disappointed that I did not go to the Bar (not that bar anyway), people like my parents did at least understand that there are many ways to find your way in life and they always reinforced the need to be happy in what you do (though I am unsure if they were happy at work themselves). And while working life is sadly not yet over for me (I would be an unashamed nightmare if I won the lottery), I can honestly say that I have been happy through the vast majority of my career. Having narrowly avoided what would have been the painful and protracted death of my soul as a lawyer, I eventually found my way into a happy and successful twenty years in sporting goods sales and marketing, confounding expectations by navigating my way to Global Sales Director level and operating most recently as Chief Commercial Officer of a very cool technology start-up with mega ambitions. That's right, I have mixed it at the top table and I need this boastful truth out there as context for what is about to follow.

And do you know what, I can finally admit to myself, that for the most part, work has gone pretty well. There will be a few people that I have helped along the way, maybe even a few more who I have inspired to do cool stuff. On the flip side there will be the inevitable group of back-stabbing shitheads who didn't like me because trying to help them be less shit was probably threatening to them. That one's a pretty long list to be fair but I am OK with that. I hope they are too. Actually, no. I couldn't care less what they think to be fair. Some shit people are destined to always be shit if their attitude surrounding their own shittery starts in a bad spot. You could say that they are so shit that they fail to recognize how shit they are in the first place.

The truth is this though. Just like for champions that work really hard at being good (and regularly fail), the effort required to be a bit less shit cannot be taken lightly either. Like any process, it needs to begin with a look in the mirror and an honest assessment of current state. "Hi, my name is David and I am shit". I haven't got charts and graphs to prove it, but I do believe that if you become less shit at something, even just a tiny bit less shit, you enjoy it more (unless you actually pride yourself on being totally shit in which case the more shit you become, the happier you are). A common view of the world would suggest that if you enjoy something, it goes hand in hand with happiness….and in the time it has taken me to complete 48 consecutive non-stop trips around the sun, I have yet to see anybody attempting to hand their happiness back because they have too much of it. Be less shit. Enjoy more. Get happy.

So, while this soon to be award winning publication is intentionally light-hearted, it is not intended to create the impression that I have made a career out of not caring or that I have not been arsed. Quite the contrary. I have only ever known what it is to work hard. I got that gene from my parents. But I have always had a perspective where work has only been a part of my life – not my whole life. It hasn't been the be all and end all and it hasn't defined who I am as an individual. My career has got me to a place where I am finally comfortable enough to share a few thoughts from the premise that I have not been totally shit at what I have done. I have learned a few bits about sales and marketing along the way and like anybody else, I have also learned from my own management and colleagues. Some of them good, some of them bad and taken all together they have unquestionably combined to help me to be a bit less shit. I didn't say good. Just a bit less shit.

In 2018 and some of 2019, I took some time off (a man needs a break from being shit sometimes) following a successful exit from a sporting goods business. This period allowed me to reflect on lessons learned over twenty years in the workplace. It also sparked this thinking about how I could pass these lessons on and position them without intimidating or overwhelming anybody who might just be trying to be a bit less shit. With such lofty aims, I hope that I have found the correct tone to facilitate the passing on of lessons learned from a career spent almost exclusively in sport. I hope as well that my learnings remain clear to you throughout, presented as they are through the media of middle-aged forgetful rambling and occasional funny stories. The expressive dance workshop remains a work in progress but we will get there and I will eventually charge you an horrendous amount of money to come and dance with me at my foreign villa while we all talk about how shit we are and sell it on to Netflix as a documentary.

My writing also coincided with a period of my girlfriend and I caring for a family member with severe mental health issues as well as trying to support elderly parents. My normally bombproof mum has confronted health challenges of her own but showed up unfailingly and unreservedly every day as the full-time carer for my dad who sadly passed away in April 2020, succumbing to coronavirus after a long battle with Alzheimer's. As they often do, genuine life or death scenarios like this never fail to offer an alternative perspective of what is really important, at the same time as taking you on your own journey in understanding how you feel about stuff. I came to accept that the situations of the people I was (and am) trying to support will each play out in their own way in the months and years ahead and if I can show up for anybody with even a fraction of the mettle that my mum brought (and brings) to her own situation on a daily basis, I will be doing okay. If my mum ever reads this, I will have to forewarn her about it being a bit sweary (she doesn't swear unless I don't do as I am told) but I would want her to know that her immense courage and strength has inspired my own thinking, not the sweary bits and not just recently, but over a lifetime. She is only small but she is immense and a hugely impressive individual.

Through this period of writing, life asked much bigger questions than anything I have ever encountered in the workplace. Perhaps deep down we all know that life isn't about deadlines, quarterly revenue targets or profit margins. Maybe it is about becoming less shit in a wider sense than you used to be and creating your own sense of self that should not be compared to that of anybody else. We all know that comparison leads you to no place worth going. Taking care of your own shit is where this all starts.

For the record, I have decided that while I would have been as entitled as the next person to offer my view on what it takes to be the best (it is just an opinion right?), my question is how many people are actually hanging on to any realistic expectation of becoming the best at what they do? Deep down I think most of us know that we are shit and it is just shades of brown that separate the majority of us. Whether it comes from a person's background or a lifetime of having it beat out of you in the workplace, the BEST is by definition the domain of the very few. For this reason, I actually quite like the expression "be the best version of yourself" (or the least shit version?), because I don't think anyone can ask any more of you than that. Naturally therefore (and like any good salesperson), when I started to think about writing this book, it was with the conscious thought of keeping my target audience as wide as possible. It is written for all of the sales muffers out there who would be even a tiny bit happier if only they could be a bit less shit.

There are lots of us out there and it should be celebrated. It certainly will be celebrated if enough of you buy this and enable me to buggar off and live abroad without having to worry about being less shit, keeping my job and getting paid regularly. And maybe that is the point. If we strip it right back to basics, most people are just trying to get through the week, or to the end of the month and another pay cheque in order to keep over-stretched lifestyles afloat. The general pattern is to repeat this until you retire and die, assuming you are lucky enough not to die first. So, before you dive into it, I just wanted to say that if this book helps you to navigate the largely inescapable routine of work and death a bit more comfortably or enjoyably, then Being Less Shit will have served its intended purpose. If it doesn't help, maybe you were already too shit for me to help and that's fine. There is no obligation to get better here and as it happens, being totally shit works for a lot of successful people, a thought I entertained for several years as we watched highly paid so-called leaders trying to negotiate Brexit while an orange gentleman on the other side of the pond completed a full term of office as President of the United States. But that is my next book – Be Less Shit At Politics.

For now, this book is about being less shit at selling stuff if you work in sales. Some of my learnings may have application beyond just sales but please accept that I am hell bent on recycling the same material and passing it off in other occupational sectors for maximum financial return at some point in the future. The villa for the expressive dance workshop is not going to pay for itself right? So for the salespeople and for now, I hope you are not too shit to actually finish the book (that would help) and if you do complete it, I wish you peace and contentment on your personal odyssey to becoming less shit. Unashamedly I have shoe-horned funny stories (well I think they are) into each chapter as a way of very tenuously illustrating my points and have taken the view that if they make my book about being less shit a bit less shit, then we all win.

SIGNS YOU MAY BE SHIT:

Before anything else, we must start the honest confessional that must accompany this process of enlightenment. Thankfully, you don't have to look too hard to find signs of shit because a lot of people that choose sales as a profession are complete shit. It is in fact a large part of the reason that sales does not have the same respect as other professions and probably never will. Eternal shitdom beckons. Don't get me wrong, every other profession will have a selection of dimwits that give a bad name to the rest – but perhaps because there are no formal entry requirements to lots of jobs in sales and because people confuse the job with just being nice to people, it is fair to say that you will see some proper shit throughout your life in sales. And your shit comes in all shapes and sizes. Just think about the double-barrel litter-runt dimwits that try to flog you a new gaff masquerading as up-market estate agents as if selling a really nice gaff is somehow difficult, the archetypal car salesmen who try to cliché you into oblivion if you haven't already killed yourself first, the furniture guy that taps away furiously on his calculator while he "works out a price". As far as I am concerned, they are an embarrassment to my chosen profession. Anyone who tells you that they can only sell at a particular price if you commit to spending thousands of pounds on the spot is a monumental douchebag. People who slag off the competition are clearly unconvinced about their own offer if they choose to denigrate somebody else's instead. More serious than anything, if a so-called salesperson can't help themselves and crosses over into the realms of dishonesty then they should be executed on the spot. These are not sales professionals. There is another word for these people but I can't write it in case my mum does actually read this book. If you are seeing signs of your own behavior here in this list, I am placing you formally on notice that it needs to stop. Immediately.

Ultimately, sales is notorious for people over-promising and leaving customers high and dry right at the point they need help (we called that a hit and run job) and dishonesty would regularly be at the origin of these shortcomings. In fact, dishonesty generally would be right up there with the list of prominent characteristics of the shittest people I have ever worked with. For me, it was always the most depressing thing to ever find out about a colleague. Thankfully, in most organisations, dishonesty has a wonderful habit of delivering its perpetrators to a point otherwise known as career end. So, before we undertake this transformation together of becoming less shit tomorrow than you are today, I will simply say that there is no place for dishonesty if you are going to move your shit slider in the right direction with my help. When it comes to dishonesty. Just don't. Please.

WHO AM I?

In an attempt to build some common ground and empathy so that the reader might enjoy this book more and buy innumerable copies for their friends because it completely changed their life (or at least validated their shitness), I was thinking that it might help if I shared a bit of my own introspection about who I am and maybe more so, who I have been in my work life. The hopefully funny stories to come are not the ramblings of a mad man – perhaps more for me the measuring stick of what I look back on as an enjoyable career to this point. But I also know that people sometimes find comfort if there are similarities between the person writing and themselves and so I will share some of what pertains specifically to me with a view to us all feeling warm and fuzzy about how shit we are.

I don't believe I have been bullied in the workplace. I have avoided that particular fate but I have certainly been around big alpha male characters all of my working life and I have been ignored by most of them. First thing to say is that this is OK. It's OK because it is not necessarily about fault and it is OK because it has been wholly my choice to work in the environments I worked in. It is also

OK because my own approach to making my point may have been flawed (my emails were always VERY long) and so being ignored may have been the natural consequence of my own shortcomings. I hold no grudges anywhere and I am simply expressing that despite what many people would regard as a successful career to date, I have been ignored and it has still all worked out fine. In the spirit of trying to be less shit (and in the face of occasionally being ignored), I can honestly say it didn't change me and I have only ever been myself in the workplace. However, while I haven't pandered to any of these individuals who might have ignored me, I have probably been overly deferential. But that is all and it hasn't proved disastrous. Thankfully, I have been fortunate enough or worked hard enough at being comfortable with myself to not worry about vying for the attention of somebody who for whatever reason decided that I wasn't worth listening to. And they may have been right. The moral for me is to not get all pissed off about it and decide that your boss is a tosser because you are unlikely to ever win from that game. Work, as in life, is a long way from a game of perfect.

In a similar related vein, I realise I have probably suffered at times from imposter syndrome. There will be all sorts of definitions of the condition but to me it is best described as the feeling you might get when you find yourself in a group of people and you start to wonder whether or not you can hold your own in their company. You start to question how you got there, whether you belong there, whether your contribution is worth anything and all of the time, these questions and doubts start to impact your thinking and behaviour. You look like a less confident individual which may be entirely justified if you are an absolute shitter and it might also be the reason why I was occasionally ignored by certain individuals wherever I have worked previously. But if anybody ever asks me today for work related advice and how they can be less shit, I urge them to think really consciously about their value and project confidently as a contributing party to whatever discussion they are a part of. There is a lot of deep science as to why this affliction might strike and a whole body of suggestion that says it will be rooted in how we were raised. A bit of that probably applies to me – coming from a working-class family that didn't really harbour any expectation of the workplace beyond it being a means to an end, we perhaps viewed ourselves for too long as service providers to large organisations instead of bona-fide contributors to the debate, thought-leaders or agents for change. Inevitably, some of that stuff rubs off. I tell anybody who cares to listen, it is important to sit your full weight at any table – even if that is light-weight shitter stakes, at least respect yourself enough to sit your full light-weight shitter weight.

The other advice I regularly offer (says he like I go about dispensing advice because my shit is so together) is about being conscious about what you do. I don't mean as opposed to unconscious because you are drunk or something. I mean that you must be conscious about what you are doing. You must be conscious about where you are, how you are doing and how long all of this will keep you in a particular role. You wont hear me talk too much about regrets because the truth is I don't have too many but if I have been guilty of anything, I stayed too long in certain posts as a loyal employee, comforted by cash and nice cars when in fact I should have pushed harder and maybe advanced more quickly. Fear not. In the context of a book about being less shit, I am not saying I should have run for PM, but let's just say I have seen one or two shitty folks in senior positions and I can't say anything or criticise because it was those people with the gumption to pursue those opportunities and I didn't. Don't get me wrong, certain appointments will always seem unfathomable and I am sure everybody can point to at least a couple where they ask "how on earth did that person get that job? He must have pictures of the boss doing something". I am not talking about that. I am talking about those occasions when an opportunity may have been perfectly suited to you but for whatever reason, you didn't see it or if you did, you didn't show up for it well enough or maybe the person who got the job was more calculating about how they got it and parked all of the self-doubt and trepidation while they told the interviewer all about being less shit than the other candidates. Meanwhile, you didn't. Some people reference the fact that what is meant to be will be, but I am not sure I subscribe to that. There is a role to fill and a variety of candidates are going to apply to fill it. Many of them will start to think about the problems that may come with a new job – for example you might need to relocate – but the calculating shitter will not harbor any of those doubts until they get the job and deal with the practicalities of it all afterwards.

A big part of what I mean when I talk about being conscious is really about having fun while you develop professionally. I don't wish to trivialise the workplace at all but if you are not having any fun at all at work then you are conceivably in the wrong gig. You might even become the unconscious worker, always bitching and moaning about their job, salary, conditions, life, existence etc and yet the truth is that very often there is only you that can do anything about that. Stop the car. Make some decisions and drive to a different destination instead of travelling every day to Shitsville on auto-pilot. It might be easier said than done but it is nonetheless true. You are going to get one go at this and it will pass by a lot quicker than you might imagine.

As I reflect on my own career, I think it would be fair to say that I have always had time for interaction with others. This is hugely important if you have set your sights on being less shit. If you give a shit about people, there is an unsurprising possibility that they will do the same for you. While you are alongside each other, they will work better with you. At a point in the future, they will take your call. I have tested this theory to destruction, and I am proud to say that fellow shitters have taken my call as I have taken theirs. Look, at the end of the day, people matter most and if you do right by them, they will invariably do right by you.

If I were to summarise how I have been over a career without too many regrets, I would simply say that I was overly deferential, didn't question enough, didn't push back enough, didn't believe enough in myself (though I was still comfortable enough with myself), didn't have a game plan soon enough and despite all of that, it has all still turned out alright. So, if your journey to being less shit has not been a perfect one, I don't think it will be unique to you and the heady heights of being a bit less shit are probably still within your grasp. If you are going to double down on your efforts, I would say trust your experience, don't let others nibble away at your confidence. You know what you have done better than anybody so have the balls to back yourself. OK, let's get started.

1. PREPARATION:

So you have all heard it a million times before. And it is still true. Preparation is the key to any level of performance. My first real boss used to hammer home the idea of the 5 P's – Proper Planning Prevents Poor Performance" and on particularly sweary days (which was every day), he made it 6 P's by inserting Piss into the mantra for added emphasis. This mantra applies as much today as ever and I dare say it always will. Even being less shit requires a level of preparation!

If I think back to my happiest occasions in the workplace or even happy encounters generally (erm, not those happy encounters), they have all been occasions where I have been properly prepared. Clearly the contrary is true where I have been unprepared for doing something, and a lack of preparation has left me anxious and unhappy. You realise over time that as you navigate the snake pits of your workplace and climb the greasy pole of corporate success, you would be incredibly lucky if you didn't encounter the back-biting shitbags who are more focused on saying the right thing to the right people at the right time than they are on actually being good at their job. Watch out for these types. They might look like your friends but there is a real chance they are not. You will realise very quickly how important being prepared is to your survival (friendly-fire is a thing) when so-called friends begin to reveal their true colours. Truth is, I have worked with people who would throw their entire family under the metaphorical (and perhaps literal) bus if it meant getting a promotion or a pay rise or a better title and let's not pretend, these shitheads are everywhere.

The sweary boss I mentioned earlier operated by what he called the 99% rule. When I first asked him what this was, he explained that 99% of people are nobheads (polite version) until proven otherwise and after twenty years in the workplace, I am delighted to tell you that he is entirely correct. So, you have been warned. Don't be fooled by somebody that seems OK because the 99% rule is unlikely to weigh in their favour. There are people in your office or place of work that will take you down at the drop of a hat but we are British and we are conditioned to not think so badly of somebody. Wise up. They are everywhere so BE PREPARED. Don't give them the chance. Be adequately prepared to do your job, that is all I am asking. Even if you are not good at what you do, you can still survive by being acceptably less shit than others. In the kingdom of the blind, the one-eyed man is king. Remember that one?

For me, while generally diligent by nature, there have been one or two episodes of unpreparedness that will probably scar me forever. At one point in my career, I used to sell very high-end golf and fitness apparel for a renowned Swedish manufacturer and as is often the case, I secured the role by virtue of being the least shit of the applicants. Recruitment is a lottery at the end of the day, no better demonstrated than an investor in my previous business who used to hold a pile of application letters over the dustbin and only interview anybody whose letter didn't fall into the bin (because "you wouldn't want to employ an unlucky person"). Incredulous but true and on this occasion, having completely fluked a brand-new job, I was not about to hand back the pay cheque. I had an overstretched lifestyle to pay for like everybody else and I had convinced myself that selling something I hadn't sold before would be no different to selling anything else. If you read no further than here, I can now confirm that this was an incorrect assumption.

I began my short tenure in this role blissfully unaware of the stark impending reality and I decided my first attempt at presenting a new high-end apparel collection could be perfected in my head over the course of a long drive to see a customer in Scotland. Back then, it was like "I mean if you can't perfect the presentation of a whole new luxury apparel collection while you are doing 85mph (ahem, 70mph) eating a fast-food dinner from your lap, are you even in sales?". I arrived in Glasgow on one of only three days in Scottish history when temperatures reached into the 30's. I fell into the trap of believing that my presentation would look even better in the reflection of people's sunny moods and that I could get away with being even more shit than I had planned to be. Despite ginger people bursting into flames all around me, everybody else was outside feeling good; the Tennent's was flowing freely and Scotland appeared determined to celebrate the fact that summer this year was on a Wednesday. Surely in the middle of all this, the last thing my customer wanted to deal with was a Sales Manager who had actually bothered to prepare for a meeting and so I convinced myself that basic shit would suffice and I would be back down the road in no time with a big fat order book. That is not exactly how the meeting played out.

My lack of preparation meant I had no idea where to park in proximity to my appointment. Thirty minutes of stressful driving around a major city centre ensued but I was at least smart enough to know beforehand that you need to be quite careful who you shout at in Glasgow, even from the safety of your own luxury German automobile. After parking, I had no idea that my sales samples and presentation kit were previously used as weights in an episode of the World's Strongest Man and I had overlooked how much I sweat when it is hot. To this day, I still look back and think that turning up for my appointment looking like the sixth member of Take That in that video where they all get drenched was not my best look. I didn't know my product particularly well (being shit doesn't include product knowledge as a pre-requisite) and yet somehow, I expected a credible established retailer to invest thousands of pounds in the range that was being presented to them by a sweaty madman.

I hadn't even considered that presenting apparel to a buyer is an art form in itself. Try for yourself to pick up an item of your own clothing and show it to a friend as though you were about to sell it to them. It is really difficult. When you see it done well, it looks good. But if you had witnessed the complete tragedy of me attempting it on that awful day, I looked like a burglar doing a runner through the backyard clothes lines of a row of terraced houses on washing day. As my presentation began, my lack of research meant my limited technique was no better than to tell a seasoned buyer what they could already see for themselves – "this is the yellow one, this is the blue one, this is the red one". I don't think this counted as "expert product knowledge" or that it would have made the top ten ranked sales presentations this buyer had ever seen and the only person to blame for that was me. Did I get the order? Did I bollocks and nor did I deserve to. On this day (and there have only been a few in my entire career), I was complete shit. Bearing in mind I had sold successfully in a different sector for ten years up to this point, this particular day had been a brutal reminder that how you sell (and how prepared you are to sell) is every bit as important as what you sell and so I headed back home down the M6 embarrassed but determined to be less shit at my next attempt. Let's face it, it couldn't get any worse.

The other thing that this day had reminded me of was not to become complacent. In selling, everybody has favourite customers and for salespeople, these are typically the customers who would buy anything from you, just because it is you. But in Scotland, I had broken one of my own golden rules by taking the situation for granted. In my previous life selling golf equipment, I had never ever taken anything for granted and so why I had attempted this new half arsed technique as an Englishman to a Scottish person I hadn't met before remains a mystery to this day (I don't know if you have heard, but one or two of them don't particularly like us). In stark comparison, I was new to selling when I sold golf equipment (my first job in sales), I was as keen as you like and within reason, customers were going to hear my pitch whether they liked it or not. Unusually for my sector, I wore a suit to my appointments and brought presentations to share on a laptop rather than in an old school folder. My future thinking back then made me look like the Elon Musk of my generation and my approach served me pretty well. In the years that followed, some of those customers made a point of saying that they respected my commitment to raising the bar (being less shit) as well as how I had respected them enough to tell them the new product story of that year or season - even though they had already told me that they were going to buy it anyway. For me, it was just a part of doing things properly. Looking back, maybe being new to something made me more prepared for those earlier meetings in my career than I had been ten years later on that day in Glasgow but regardless of the reason, Scotland had served as a harsh reminder that the need to always be prepared never goes away, no matter how experienced and acceptably shit you had been in any former life.

Different people will of course have their own view on preparation and when it comes to people, I can honestly say that I have been lucky enough to work with all sorts of shit. Some colleagues who were very shit, others were a lot better by virtue of being just shit and then there were the best, who I thought of in terms of being the least shit. If I placed you in my "least shit" category, it was more than likely to be the result of my admiration for the way you prepared. I have always said that sales is a very easy job to do badly but a very difficult job to do well and the least shit guys I have worked alongside have tended to be the most prepared. It might be how prepared they were for a meeting or perhaps how prepared they were to use their own time to wrap things up after a meeting. Bottom line, they were more prepared and therefore less shit than others, they earned more money and wore better clothes. They generally also had bigger watches which back then (and still now) would be considered the salesperson badge of honour! Like I have said, it was about who could be the least shit and while this was an accolade that only some of us dared to dream of, the truth is that for many, being less shit than others who were complete shit was the absolute pinnacle of a career. Heady heights indeed!

In any sales group, you tend to get lots of strong personalities and a high percentage of them would assume they were fully prepared because in their heads, they knew everything there was to know about everything. If you were one of these types, there was nothing left for you to learn (because you were a complete shitter) and it is tragically remarkable how prevalent this was in every organisation I have ever worked in. If we were preparing for a sales drive, these would be the guys who wouldn't listen during presentations, sounding off about inconsequential shit and disrupting meetings (you know the type), and their slubbornly body language would suggest anything but interest from the outset. They were also the same people who called up five minutes after a meeting to go back over things that had already been discussed and unsurprisingly, they were the same people who were fired when the first recession of my professional life came knocking in 2008. You have heard of survival of the fittest. This was soon to become death of the shittest and I would imagine that for many companies, even as they teetered on the brink of their existence, there must have been genuine delight for many at the prospect of being able to clear out their shitters (so to speak) and have another go at creating the least shit team possible. On occasions, shitters who were gotten rid of attempted to blame their shitness on others by claiming they were bullied, put under duress or pressured by performance management. I would venture to suggest that this pattern of feeble nonsense was (and is) repeated the world over in organisations where performance levels are ranked and unfathomably (at least for the shittest), you are held accountable for your results. I mean who would have thought that in return for your salary and fancy car that there would be an expectation of you to prepare properly to do your job and to be accountable for results? There is always an excuse for those people that can't quite get it done but don't let emotional retorts distract you from the truth. Sales is good for lots of reasons, not least because it leaves shitters nowhere to hide if they are unwilling to prepare properly and try to become even a bit less shit.

I will indulge myself here for a moment to share with you the story of a Scottish rep on my team (and if he happens to buy this book, he will know instantly who he is) and he had it in him to be a really painful bastard on occasions...about the only thing he was good at. If I said black, he said white. If there were no holidays during busy periods, he would attempt to book time off. If there were reasons to be hopeful and optimistic, he would be the mood-hoover that brought everybody down. If you gave him a fifty-pound note, it was wrong because it should have been five tens. You know the type. He was one of those Godforsaken people who was only happy when he was unhappy. I heard in later years that he had struggled in various respects and while I wouldn't wish suffering on anybody, the thought crossed my mind many times that his suffering might have been some form of payback for the suffering he had inflicted on others. I am a karma guy and I knew all along that his day would come, and it did. Sitting across the desk from him as we fired him will remain a career memory for me as I had nothing left to give him emotionally. Literally nothing. Perhaps incorrectly on my part, I made a particular point of sitting slumped in my chair as I gave him the good news, mimicking the way he had slumped in his chair during every presentation that either myself (or anybody else) had ever given as his manager. That is just how angry and frustrated I felt about him. My point is that in sales, his approach gets you nowhere. Don't be that guy. Don't be total shit. There is absolutely a point to trying to be less shit. Remember, a lot of people work hard behind the scenes to enable a sales force in any company. You need to demonstrate respect for this at all times and prepare properly to do the job you are paid to do. People in any business talk to each other and it would be nice if the conversation of others at the water fountain was about how you were the least shit in a large group of shitters instead of a massive shitter. Being aware of this and respectful of it goes a long way and you will each of you know where you are on that line.

To finish the point on preparation, there is always something to learn in sales to become better prepared and the least shit people I have worked with conducted themselves according to this belief. It is too easy to fall into lazy habits after years on the road and as your energy diminishes over time, while you might not detect your own decline, your customers will. I had the highest performing sales territory in my country at one point in my career and could legitimately claim to have been less shit than at least one or two of my colleagues. But I knew my energy for the area was waning, I was becoming shitter and it was time to hand it over to somebody younger and less shit who came on to my territory with new energy and took it to even greater heights. I would be delighted every day of the week to be outperformed by this particular individual because he was a great example of wanting to be the least shit of us all. From day one, when the league tables went up on the big screen, he was in the ear of the leaders telling them how he was less shit than they were and would be sitting above them very soon. And to be fair, he backed it up. He made a very clear signal that he was less shit than everybody else and quickly assumed the mantle of the least shit person in our group. I am delighted to say that he remains a great friend and has gone on to do truly great things.

To close this chapter, I wanted to share something I picked up from a documentary I watched featuring a former special-forces operative and his journey to conquer Everest. Somebody he passed on the way up wished him luck for the ascent whereupon the Operative's response was a stone cold "luck is for the unprepared". It stopped me dead in my tracks. "Luck is for the unprepared". It was akin to the old saying in golf that "the more I practice, the luckier I get". I think the takeaway here is simple. Better to be prepared than to rely on being lucky. You can be less shit if you prepare properly.

2. RELATIONSHIPS

There is the very well-known adage in sales that people buy from people. This is really a euphemism for saying that relationships are very often at the heart of what you are able to accomplish in sales. Having done it for twenty years, I would agree with this point of view and while I wouldn't say that they are everything, they are a major factor in determining whether you will succeed or fail on your chosen path. People would regularly reference a salesperson as having "the gift of the gab" but this is quite demeaning to a professional salesperson as to me it diminishes a much greater skill than just being good at talking. A salesperson's relationships are unquestionably built on an ability to communicate however there are many more aspects to success than just talking a good game.

The other part of this is how well a salesperson is able to adapt their style and presentation depending on who it is they are dealing with. The shit guys tend to overlook this fact and just blurt out whatever is on their laptop screen in a robotic style where style, sales craft and finesse have no part to play. It was my number one pet peeve on sales manager accompaniments to see salespeople sounding off without even noticing that their customer had stopped listening a long time ago. I remember being on a visit to see customers in Ireland with a team member I was managing at the time and who was actually really successful at selling over time. When he was new to his role, he had turned up at a very old school golf course with a very old school and utterly wonderful club pro to try and sell his wares. On my visit, the pro was relaying the story of how our guy had turned up there several years earlier and having begun his presentation, he just kept going and going and going and going. If you can imagine a West of Ireland accent, the pro said to me he decided to leave the room and went out to give a few lessons to his members and when he returned to his shop several hours later, he said "your man was still going and I wasn't sure he had even noticed that I had been out!". Now this story may have grown arms and legs but if you are in sales, you will have seen it and perhaps done it and it has no place in a strategy to become less shit. If less shit is where you are heading, then you will realise quickly that you have two ears and one mouth for good reason. Be sure to use them in that ratio.

For me, it was apparent quite quickly that, especially in a social industry like sporting goods, relationships and an ability to forge and foster them would have a huge say in my success or failure. In one of my early roles, I used to deal with golf magazines, a number of whom were based about thirty minutes from our offices in a place called Peterborough. I think I can get away with telling this story now because things in that sector have changed so much over twenty years, but our arrangement used to be that we could go and sit in their offices, write our own articles for publication (funny how my products never had a bad write-up!) on the proviso that we would take the journalists and title big-wigs to get pissed afterwards. I am not sure if it still happens, but back then there was the Peterborough beer festival and I was attending with a collection of journalists (who it was important to have good connections with) and the plan was to do the normal thing and get them absolutely wasted. I was with my then boss who has gone on to occupy a very senior position with a major industry brand and let's just say that he had a reputation for enjoying himself in his earlier years at every available opportunity. And I am easily led. Strong combo. On this particular evening, we had set ourselves the ambitious task of impersonating beer festival staff which required us to climb the steel rigging that held hundreds of barrels of beer and cider high in the air. Rather than queue up like normal people, we would climb up and move along the rigging, tap on each barrel as if we were doing something super hi-tech to check the contents and while nobody was looking (or so we thought) we would take a sip from each of them. Needless to say, that by the time we got to the end of the line, we were in a state I will describe here as "judgement impaired". When you achieve this higher state of unconsciousness, it regularly coincides with that point in the evening that will be familiar to many - that point where the only possible way things could get any better is to round off proceedings by committing some sort of crime. I don't think either of us will go down in history as a criminal mastermind but what mattered is that at the time and in our heads, we were the great train robbers, Brinks Mat, Hatton Garden all rolled into one. For one night only, we were the Peterborough mafia.

After a highly detailed planning meeting (well, as detailed as it could be after twenty pints of strong continental loopy juice), we hatched a plan that would go down in history as one of the greatest criminal heists in the Peterborough area that week. The bizarre beer festival novelty shop was going to become the target of our criminal endeavour and we had decided that if we were going to risk doing time for something then the potential reward had to be significant. Guided by this thought, my friend set his sights on a life size cardboard cutout of Barney Rubble from the Flintstones and after careful deliberation, I had decided that I was going to try and relieve the fancy goods emporium of a six-foot-tall inflatable penis. I don't suppose that we looked like stealthy ninjas at this point in the proceedings and security had clearly locked on to this criminal Laurel and Hardy without us noticing. Their strategy seemed to be a case of selecting the easiest target which meant jumping on the little fat lad and sadly for yours truly, that meant me! In the situation, I was relieved to learn that my really good friend did exactly as you would hope in a moment of total need and worsening crisis – which was to run in the complete opposite direction at full pelt towards the high security perimeter fencing. While I wrestled on the ground with two or three security guards and a giant inflatable penis (I know, it was a classy event), I could still see my friend making a valiant bid for freedom that wouldn't have been out of place in the Great Escape. There is no real need to go into any more detail in a sales guide but for anybody interested in how the story ended, I was eventually able to get free of the large appendage and three fat blokes marauding all over me. When I eventually made it to the outside, more trouble beckoned as my friend and Barney Rubble were pissing off all the taxi drivers at the rank, asking them how much it would cost to get back to Bedrock. While I wouldn't advocate a life of crime to build good relations with your customers or your particular audience, the moral of the story is that these were the things that people talked about for years afterwards and probably still do to this day. Well, I do anyway.

Bring this all back to where it started, if you are going to be less shit at sales, there will be occasions when you are going to have to dig deep and consider your relationship with your customers and other vested interests in ways that go beyond the strict content of your job description. My employment contract didn't make any reference to penis theft or whatever else went on that night, but it was clear to me very quickly that succeeding in my role was going to go well beyond just doing what I did in the office. It would become true of my entire career and the standout characters from a long list of former colleagues would all bear the hallmark of that willingness to invest time in the relations they had with their customers. This is a big part of why I say sales is an easy job to do badly and a really difficult job to do well. It wont always fit with your own plans or your family time or you might not even like the customer you are doing it for, but the basic premise is that you need to remain open-minded to this being a part of your career in sales. Relationships need to be built and that is not always convenient.

At this point and in the context of forming good relations, it is often built on an ability to adjust your style according to who you are stood in front of. You probably wouldn't take an up-market strait-laced hard-nosed no-nonsense all-business kind-of-a-customer to the Peterborough Beer Festival, but part of the skill of becoming less shit at sales is getting to know your customer as an individual.

Everybody has motivating factors in life and finding out what these are – their hot buttons if you like - can work wonders in building a relationship. This point is not intended to suggest that you should be in any way disingenuous about who you are and say stuff just because you think it will get you your result, that approach will be found out very quickly. But when all said and done, if you are interested in others at the same time as being comfortable enough to be yourself, you won't go far wrong.

We are led to believe that something like 75% of buying decisions are made on an emotional basis and then justified afterwards with logic. This in itself tells you that you are going to have to deliver more than a bone-dry product presentation and that at some point, relationships are going to come into it. With good relations comes trust and that trust drives loyalty. You might be reading this thinking it is obvious but if you have ever tried to recruit a salesperson from a rival brand and called around some of their customers to see who is any good on a sales area, you will also know that very few customers have a long list of trusted salespeople that they would recommend. If you can be one of the names that your customer is happy to volunteer when somebody asks for a recommendation, you are already doing yourself a massive career favour. Sadly (or gladly for you if you are less shit than others), because most people are shit at the job, it doesn't actually take a whole lot to be shortlisted as a trusted sales ninja. I should know.

Based on my experience, lack of trust in sales is driven by people who seem to want to try and please everyone all of the time and to do that they overpromise, regularly under-deliver and sometimes try to become somebody that they are not. They think that by saying yes to everything, you are going to get your best possible result, but it doesn't work that way and we will cover that in another chapter. Setting yourself up to disappoint your customers is stupid but we are talking about your average shitters here and so perhaps we shouldn't be surprised. Relationships are at the very centre of your working life in sales and I can certainly speak from experience when I say that my relationships got me through long periods of the 2008-2013 downturn as well as stages in my career when I have sold what can best be described as me-too products. I was under no illusion that people were buying from me precisely because it was from me. Don't overlook this fact (it certainly helps) but don't be lulled either into a false sense of security that it will be this way forever. Nurture and cherish these relationships and you will be putting yourself ahead of a fair majority of your sales peer group.

3. OPPORTUNISM:

Early in my selling career, I had just left an appointment and when I got back into my car, I took a call from a retailer who was probably thirty minutes away from my current location. He had called up to bitch and moan about never seeing a sales rep from my then employer and in so doing, he served me up a gilt-edged opportunity to win him round. I was new to the area and didn't really feel any sense of responsibility for what had happened in the past however I did accept that I was now entirely responsible for where this discussion would go from here. "I can be with you in thirty minutes" I said and as it happens, the person in question had a gap in his diary and was happy to meet on the spot. At the time, our biggest product package was £4000 which back then for a me-too brand was a fairly meaty investment. Within a couple of hours of my arrival, I had established a relationship and demonstrated an enthusiasm to do business such that a conversation which had started out as a complaint only hours earlier turned into a deal that would signal the start of a decent business relationship for years to come. The point is that opportunities are all around you and it is how you deal with them that governs where you are on the shit scale. While this particular example was a chance event, the truth is that the least shit people I have worked with over a lifetime have nearly always built time into their schedule to prospect for new customers. At the time it seems like you are taking your eye off the ball in regard to everything else you might have on your plate and there is never a good time to do that right? But, if you go to this process with a structure and you plan for it in advance, you can be organized enough to explore future opportunity at the same time as you are taking care of your day-to-day business. Opportunities are out there. In fact, they are everywhere. Even in France.

I had once been on a flight to Paris to attend a training session with a good friend and colleague (the same guy that undresses for me in a later chapter – I know, the literary equivalent of clickbait). We were going to do some work with an individual that neither of us cared much for (a condescending Parisian!) and as if the prospect of a day in the classroom with this guy was not already too much to cope with, we ended up with front row seats at the serious unravelling of a gentleman who appeared to be having a serious cardiac episode 30,000 feet away from help. A commotion was developing on the seats directly across from us and I could make out that the individual had started to sweat profusely, almost as if a tap had emerged from the top of his head and started pouring out. In true Hollywood style, there were chest grabs, panicked neighbours and the disturbingly absent "highly trained" cabin crew who clearly had no idea what to do next in this gentleman's moment of dire need. To cap it off, we arrived at Paris and in true French "we will get to it in our own time" style, we were told that there would be a ten-minute delay before we could access our stand. That's right. Just when you think an emergency protocol would get you directly to a team of highly trained medical professionals who would jump into action and save your life, it seems the chances are that you will be forced to wait and disembark in a manner that suits French flight controllers more than it suits your failing vital organs. But I digress, this is not the story of opportunism. What follows is opportunism of a magnitude you have never seen before.

As the drama on the flight unfolded in front of us, my colleague began to recount the story of a time he had been on a plane when a passenger actually succumbed to a condition and died. "Oh yes mate, this stuff happens all the time when I am around" he began to tell me. "People become unwell around me and in one instance a passenger even died. Seriously mate, all the time it happens. Whenever I fly, shit goes down". I was tapping away furiously on my laptop, cranking out a draft email to the lady that organized our travel to make sure that I never flew alongside this great friend and former colleague ever again. But for now, I had no choice and he went on with his story. I must admit, I was intrigued as to what really does happen when a person dies on a plane. My friend explained that the person was bagged up, dragged down the aisle and laid peacefully to rest in one of the storage areas at the front normally reserved for the pilot's jacket. "What!" I said. "What the hell did you do while this was going on?". My good friend went on...

"Well the first thing I did was find out if he was having chicken or fish". After a moment, I assumed that my friend had been trying to figure out whether this person had perished as a result of something he had eaten but I couldn't have been any further from the truth. "No, no, no. Not that at all. This was back when lunch had been pre-ordered and given that we were now one man down, there was a meal going spare and it had my name all over it!". Holy shit. Can you believe it? Opportunism, the likes of which I had not seen either before or since. I actually told this story to a large group at a sales gathering and challenged the collective masses to demonstrate opportunism like this as they set about their new campaigns. Turning a death into a free meal was a more extreme example of turning my complaining customer's negative into a positive, but the point is the same. Opportunity really is all around you and if you want to be even a bit less shit, you can tap into it safe in the knowledge that most of your shit colleagues won't be. Anyone can deal with what is in front of them but separation of abilities really starts to happen when you turn around somebody who might have had a bad previous experience with your product or brand (or when you get a spare meal from a dead guy). One of my old managers used to say that "selling begins when the need to sell outweighs the need to buy" and this strikes me still today as a fairly faithful portrayal of what the sales process is all about. For me it links to opportunity and a salesperson's ability to portray a sale as an opportunity that will benefit both parties to the negotiation. Looking back, whether it is deals I have done myself or perhaps team members who have come to me with ideas, the least shit people have always ventured into the area of opportunity as a point of difference with the complete shitters who would never do an ounce more than what was put in front of them. If you like sport, you can appreciate the analogy that champions are typically those that make opportunity or take opportunity when it presents itself. The also-rans tend to talk in terms of "would have, could have, should have" but sadly for most of them, they didn't and don't.

4. BUSINESS TRAVEL AND WORKING AWAY FROM HOME:

It is a safe assumption that if you are going to work in sales and must travel to see customers, then you should prepare yourself for periods away from home. You know this in advance and for anybody that has a problem with it, my advice would be to pack your big boy pants (or big girl pants or non-binary pants or whatever pants you wear) and just get on with it. In my experience, people who have fallen into my less shit bracket and done OK for themselves have all spent periods of time away from home to complete their work (whether they wanted to or not) and generally succeeded at what they do. It is unfathomable to me the number of people I have encountered who get all pissed off about having to stay occasional nights in hotels on an all-expenses paid basis. In my own background, for colleagues it regularly included being taken overseas to play a bit of golf and enjoy a few beers with your workmates and somehow the shitters still found reason to complain! I have heard it all. "The greens are a bit slow. The wi-fi is tricky. My room is a bit far from reception". Etc,etc, etc. When you think about it, these trips more often than not, give rise to some great adventures and they can be the things that bond colleagues more tightly together than anything else. It is just a question of how you cope with it.

I have travelled a lot with work, and I will say it, it wasn't ever my most favourite thing but I have a million great memories of things that happened on a professional basis as well as on a personal basis as a result of time spent with colleagues. If you want to break it down and think about it logically, you are living at the expense of your company, you get to stay away from your partner (which is useful if you don't like them. Not me. I love mine.) and you hang around in restaurants and bars, flicking through your social media on your phone (or rightmove) while you sit next to other folks who are doing exactly the same thing. You sleep in your own bed undisturbed by kids (if you have them), someone else's bed (if you are that way inclined and many former colleagues were!) and you can wake up the next day and put your coffee and pain au chocolat on your expenses. In today's world of social media, you can even take a photograph of it and try to convince your mates that you are "living your best life". Apparently.

Some of my best memories involve my flight buddy from the dead person story and I was lucky enough to travel with him a fair few times. I will describe him as a good, honest Yorkshireman, rambunctious and great fun to spend time with. He had set me straight a few times on my own journey to being less shit and I think you must value that trait in anybody, that willingness to tell you something that you might not necessarily like to hear. We would become genuine friends over time and on this particular occasion, we were rooming together in the "courting" stages of our relationship when I still wasn't quite sure if he was a keeper.

We were at The Open championship which to non-golfers is a major tournament in the sport and held once a year in July. It was taking place in Scotland and we had been present at a product launch during the early evening ahead of what was likely to become a night of copious boozing and debauchery. There is no point in pretending, that is just how it was on work trips. Well, it tended to be that way on my work trips. Then, the older you get, the better you deal with it. Over the years I have seen some right states and been in a few as well. At this particular event and unusually for me, I was starting to feel quite ill (medically, not self-inflicted) and the feeling was becoming worse as the product launch went on. I decided that it made more sense for me to pull the cord and bail out of the drunken carnage that was sure to follow. I went happily back to my bed at our hotel digs and tried desperately to sleep before the revellers returned. Unable to get rest due to a hacking cough and high temperature, I was going through that process where the harder you try to sleep, the harder it becomes to actually do until you eventually realise that it is futile. I heard our Tour guys return first (our earliest risers tended to be in bed first) and it would have been early hours by the time "Hurricane Roomie" hit land. The front door slammed, anything left within arms reach in the kitchen went flying and the door to our bedroom nearly came off its hinges. Did I really just say that being away from home with work could be good fun!!!

Now let me be absolutely clear at this point. I am talking here of a fine gentleman, a silhouette finely chiselled from a lifetime's monastic commitment to corporate hospitality and employer's expense accounts (he would crack me up rubbing his belly and telling me it was a "fuel tank on a love machine"). It took him the grand total of about two weeks to corrupt me when we first met (I already told you I am easily led) and being with him in a corrupt place was always a happy place to be. Except for the hangovers. I met him for the first time a few weeks before I was going to tackle the Manchester Marathon and I was fit. But after a night out with him, I was often fit for sod all, but I was a willing accomplice. He was and still is much loved everywhere he went or goes but on this particular evening, he was about to perpetrate one of the most terrifying ordeals of my entire life. I have since opened my heart and found forgiveness for what happened there that night but the therapy is ongoing. He bowled into our room, arms aloft like he had just scored the winning goal in the cup final, announcing his return at a volume level that suggested the virtual removal of the bedroom door hadn't already been enough to wake me (and half of Scotland). And then the nightmare began. "Come on Pritch, let's have it" he boomed out in deepest Yorkshire!! Now I consider myself a man of the world but at that particular point I was unsure what it was my friend wanted to "have" and I was even less sure about whether or not I was going to give it to him. The routine began with him removing his trousers over his shoes in a manoeuvre that Houdini would have been proud of. Then the shirt came off, swiftly followed by the underpants but black socks and shoes were staying on to complete a fairly unique look. Over the years, I have heard other people recount tales of great drama where their lives have flashed before them in some kind of suspended animation and that is how this felt, thinking all the time to myself that this was not how I had thought my life would end. I was afraid to even move which meant I couldn't reach for the standard hotel issue bedside notepad to scribble a tragic farewell to my friends and family. As events played out, my friend and colleague swayed around the room with his considerable appendage very close to invading my personal space until he eventually keeled over onto his bed and in a heartbeat, he fell straight asleep. In the blink of an eye, as quickly as it had begun, the terror stopped.

Why am I telling you this? Part of succeeding in sales is becoming battle-hardened over time and I don't limit that process of battle-hardening to just those things that happen while you are sat at a desk or in front of a customer. Travel is part of life in sales and the stuff that regularly happens on work trips will forge your experience in ways you never imagined. I would go as far to say that work travel is a rite of passage and your sales stripes are only earned when you have embraced this way of life and established your own way of dealing with it. For me, my approach was to embrace it, I over-indulged on occasions but I had accepted it as part of what I did. In later life, I managed myself according to a stricter regime where I would pay more attention to what I ate and on occasions, I would introduce exercise where it was possible to do so. It became an occasion for me to get good sleep as well as some inevitable evening hours staying on top of my work in a spirited attempt to be less shit. And I would say that my experience was fairly typical. The people that embraced the role including travel were the people that tended to succeed. I am not saying you should expect to have to go out and get pissed every night on expenses, in fact much of that sort of behaviour has been stamped out. But if I think back, people who didn't last the course in a group tended to keep themselves on the outside, tended to be the ones that moaned about being away or invented excuses to try and be excused from travel. I suppose it is a demonstration of reluctance and a resistance to truly become a part of the group. Perhaps the moral of the story is that being enthusiastic about what's in front of you will often help you in your quest to be less shit. This is a good example of what I said in the foreword that lessons here may have application beyond just sales. Let's face it, if you go to anything with enthusiasm and swim with the tide instead of against it, you tend to be better received as a result and you are more likely to succeed. If you are having to force that enthusiasm on these occasions, I would be asking myself if I was in the right chosen profession.

For me I think I did choose the right profession and I don't really have many regrets (if any). Writing a book is however perhaps a good opportunity to confess (not an individual crime) but that a group I was once a part of did in fact commit what would be considered the ultimate violation of a group's code if we had been in the military – we did the unthinkable and we left a man behind. We had been in Spain for a sales meeting and the last night ended up as the usual free for all beer and wine swilling schmozzle. We were all still the worse for wear when an early coach came to transport us all to the airport the following morning. You might take the view that you are in the big school and that you need to account for your own movements, to be where you need to be and to be there on time. That said, we were all friends and even if we were all at different points on the shit spectrum, we let our colleague down big time. For the sake of the story, we will call our colleague Jonesy (because his second name was Jones) and let's just say he enjoyed two things in abundance back then. Let's just say those things were beer and sleep. Let's also say that this is not a good combination when your bus is leaving early for the airport after an evening on the smash. It wasn't until we were starting our descent into London Luton airport that somebody first asked, "Where's Jonesy?". It is funny looking back now but at the time we all went sheet white as we realised we had left one of our own behind. I had taken on the role of managing a few of the team members by then and I had to give off the company line that every man was responsible for his own movements and to be where he needed to be on time. The whole thing perhaps spoke more to the horrendous state we were all in to not notice that a member of our small group hadn't made the flight with us and was sleeping soundly in his bed back at the hotel just as our plane touched down in our home country. Anyway, you have been warned. Shit happens on these excursions and you need to be ready for it.

5. PARETO

Many of you will be familiar with the very regular reference to Pareto in business and the idea that 20% of your customers might generate 80% of your business. It clearly varies depending on your sector but it is a pretty good rule of thumb and regardless of the exact percentages, the principle holds good. This is the bit where somebody normally says "yes, well we know that" and it is generally a shitter who has just put themselves right in my line of fire by more than likely being totally unaware of how and where they spend their time as a sales person.

A secret enemy in sales is the temptation to spend time with customers that you like, regardless of how much money they spend with you. I am going to say right now that I have done this myself. Sometimes I needed to do it for my sanity and other times it was a lack of structure on my part or perhaps a level of over-ambition to try and generate turnover where it didn't realistically exist. That all said, regardless of the reasons, this is a confessional on my part before I earn back the right to call you a plant pot if you have been guilty of the same thing yourself (don't say as I do, do as I say right?). Truth is, it is very easy to do because sales is very often a lonely road and as human beings, we crave company and especially so if you are having a shitty day or perhaps feeling the pressure a bit from a psychopathic manager.

In my first week in sales, I was bungling my way around a strange territory, my journey planning was horrendous and I was probably late that week for every appointment I made. It was winter selling season, I had been thrown in at the deep end and on this particular day, it was freezing cold, pissing down, pitch black and I was ninety minutes late for what should have been a four 'o' clock meeting. It didn't help that I was driving around the depths of the countryside in Warwickshire and sat nav was something you only saw on BBC's Tomorrow's World (if you are old enough to know what that is). But I did have an enormous mobile phone which took up most of the passenger seat and I had called ahead to inform my customers (a golf club near Stratford-upon-Avon) that I would be late. Amazingly, they were very relaxed about the whole thing. I was up the other end of that particular relaxation scale, being late never sat well with me and still doesn't to this day. But do you know what? As stupid as this might sound, when I got there, the club professional and his two assistants had waited for me, slipped into their rain hats made by the brand I was representing at that time and had come out to meet me in the car park while they performed a dance routine they had clearly been working on for some time. As the rain fell across my headlights as I drew into their car park, I can't tell you how relieved I was to eventually get there and how welcome I was made to feel with their crackpot antics. In I went, we did some business and it was the start of a great relationship right there. Sadly, the pro is question went on to demonstrate that he was better at crazy dancing than retail but there were a handful more just like him who were easy to be around even if the financial return didn't always justify the time spent there. Another favourite (who will clearly remain nameless) eventually became another who ran into financial challenges and even though in my head I knew he was struggling, in my heart I wanted him to win and he was good for my soul. So, I continued to call there even though I nearly always left without an order. He always did what he could if he had spare cash to spend with me but he became another one where in the strictest professional sense, I over-invested my time spent versus financial return. But I I didn't regret a minute. I mainly went there because he was just great fun to be around. One of his things was "the bucket run". On shitty weather days when nothing much was happening in the shop, we would toss a coin to see who would scoot down to KFC for the family bucket deal, a pre-requisite before we could even think about any high-level business chat. I would imagine that Jobs, Gates, Branson et al all prepared for their high level meetings in exactly the same way.

Probably my favourite was the time I arrived somewhere else (Surrey) and an anonymous customer (for obvious reasons) was stood behind his counter wearing a lady's thong over his face. Yes, it is not regular protocol for your standard business meeting but it was standard for here and I absolutely loved it. The thong was in fact one of a collection he kept in his golf bag, all of which were a souvenir from "special" female pupils and a "rewarding" career spent teaching ladies how to swing it. So to speak. It was another guy who spent almost nothing with me over the years but he and his thongs never failed to turn a shitty day into a better one.

OK, so getting back to Pareto and the principle is simple if you are still reading and still remotely interested in being less shit. It starts with knowing how many working days there are at your disposal in a calendar year. Most shitters jump in at this point and say "well it is 365 minus weekends minus holidays" – which if we use 104 days for weekends and 33 for holidays including public holidays as an average, we are left with 228 right? Wrong. You can also factor in any or all of the following: 2 x car service days, 4 sick days, 4 shit just came up days, 8 days for sales meetings, 2 days for training, 2 days at the office because somebody there needs your help, 2 days per month at home to make appointments (so 24 days) – that is another 46 days to come off 228 which leaves us with 182. There will be other distractions but you get the general idea and when you really deep dive this stuff, you wonder how you actually have any time left to do your job. When you bottom this out relative to your own situation, you need to work out how many sales calls per day you carry out on average (which isn't simple because it varies depending on time of year), multiply this by the number of available days and this gives you your total call capacity. Let's say your call capacity is 350 visits per year, and that with a car and benefits and N.I etc, you cost your employer £70,000 to be on the road, you can see that every visit you make costs £200 BEFORE you sell a thing. Finally, you need to decide how many visits per annum you would like to allocate to each customer. It doesn't matter which industry you are a part of, the bottom line is that you probably have insufficient time to do your job and you definitely do if you spend time with people who perform rain dances in Warwickshire or wear ladies thongs on their head (err, somewhere in Surrey and that is as much as I am saying).

The other really cool thing with this analysis is that one of your team shitters will always pipe up and say that what you are telling them is obvious and that they themselves would never spend time with time-wasters. My advice is to always challenge that person back if you are less shit than them and know anything about their area. I used to ask that person flat out how many times they had seen "Bob" this year (who spends thruppence halfpenny) and the really shit ones always say they "don't really see Bob" – and go on to say "I only went to drop off a gift, and then I went there to resolve a missing shipment, oh – and then I needed to pick up a return from there because he was having a head-off". All of a sudden, you have managed to confirm your own shitness to your manager because not really seeing Bob turns out to actually mean that you have seen him three times already this year at a cost of £200 per visit. Here is the truth. If it was your own money and you weren't too shit to realise, you wouldn't do it would you? You wouldn't spend £600 on a customer that spends £100 per year with you and spends the rest of his time bitching about how shit you are. Don't get me wrong, Bob is correct. You are shit. But you don't need to continue to burn your company's cash to prove him right. Time is money. Think carefully about how and where you spend it.

Ultimately, I suppose it is all part of the wider discussion and the saying I have heard many times in sales "What gets measured gets done". For the record, I believe this is absolutely true. In the same way the Pareto analysis measures where you are spending your time and enables you to act based on your findings, the truth is that anything that is measured occupies a different place in your brain. In the period of time off I enjoyed through 2018 and 2019, I ran almost every day and recorded my miles religiously in a little book. I achieved my goals (decent weight loss and a clear enough mind to write this nonsense) and I was very pleased with myself. Then as I started to think about work and one or two other (granted major) events began to dominate my calendar, I noticed that the discipline of writing down my miles was slipping. You might argue it was because I was doing less of them and it looked less impressive on the page and that then became a death spiral. The point is that I went from a steady 25-30 miles per week average back down to almost nothing because I had lost the discipline and then the buzz of keeping myself honest. I wasn't writing them down so I became less bothered about doing them. I had gone from needing to complete every step of my weekly intended mileage so that I could fill out my little book and smile at myself to writing down nothing because it had got away from me and I didn't care enough anymore. Having lost thirty pounds and then subsequently put it all back on, I can't tell you how frustrated I am, especially when I am as experienced in reporting disciplines as I am. Still, I suppose that less shit is a journey, not a destination – at least that is what I keep telling myself. The moral: write it down (shit, that is a big number), be honest with yourself (I don't really suit XXL), do the analysis (I can be fit again in three months), act accordingly (get your lazy arse up and out for a run). You get the drift. Similarly, I have seen Bob sixteen times this year, Bob has spend £37 with me, my visits have cost my company £3200, I need to see Bob less. Easy really.

6. TRADE SHOW FEVER: - what has this got to do with being less shit?

I thought long and hard about whether or not to include this as its own section (arguably, it could have been included as part of the chapter on business travel) but I have decided it should have its own space as a sort of one-man campaign to highlight the growing problem of a little-talked-about condition very prevalent in sales and known as trade show fever. It is a deadly condition and can strike at any time but normally after a salesperson has been present at a trade show or exhibition for a number of days consecutively. The consequences are potentially fatal (I shit you not shitters) and as such, I think it is good if we can open up and at least provide an environment for people to talk about it. I have seen a number of colleagues struck down by it over the years and it is a non-discriminatory condition. It can affect total shitters, average shitters and even your best shit from a bad bunch and characteristic of its impact, it can be gone almost as soon as it arrives. Symptoms vary but they can include tiredness, uncontrollable laughter, inability to construct coherent sentences, monumental piss-taking (either of each other or better still, customers) and sometimes a very delusional sense of needing to cause trouble for your colleagues at the same time as completely forgetting the professional reasons you are at the event in the first place. In short, while it lasts, it is a debilitating condition with no known cure and worryingly, experts say that it is on the increase.

My own worst episode of the condition was at The Open Championship in 2005, a monumental event in golf, especially as it was going to be the final Open Championship of legendary golfer, Jack Nicklaus. Eight or nine days into my stint away from home and with sporting history being written all around me at the home of golf, the condition struck me down on the final day of the tournament. Just as my mind needed to remain laser focused on the unravelling of the event, I developed instead (without any warning) an overwhelming sense of mischief and a need to get one of my colleagues into some seriously deep shit. This wouldn't be my normal character but the condition takes no prisoners (said he, absolving himself of all responsibility for what's about to follow) and like I said, it has an almost paranormal capability of making you do things that you normally wouldn't. Honest. From a public health perspective, it is important to pass on the learning about when and how these episodes can manifest and so for no greater purpose than the health and wellbeing of the entire planet, I have decided to use this platform to open up and share how it happened to me.

It was Sunday, we were all ready to go home after a long nine-day stint and I was on our exhibition stand with an I.T colleague whose nickname was Percy. He was great fun (he made up for being ginger by having a great sense of humour) and the fact we let him out of the cage occasionally where we kept the other I.T people spoke volumes for how highly we thought of him. He was shy but after nine days he plucked up the courage to tell me that he rather liked the look of one of the ladies on the stand directly across from ours, belonging to the Royal and Ancient Golf Club of St Andrews. Kind (bastard) that I am, I offered to relay this message to the object of his growing ardour but Percy seemed slightly reluctant (he actually begged me not to). The fever does not care remotely for the reluctance of a good colleague and forced me instead into pressurising Percy with an ultimatum – namely that he needed to approach the young lady himself or I was going to do so on his behalf. Like I said, it is a brutal condition when it strikes. Percy said no but I consider myself a man of my word and thought I would make my approach regardless. I approached this woman's friend and focusing solely on Percy's strengths, I moved in to tell her that the ginger guy sweating profusely on our stand fancied her mate and I asked if she could let her know. She shut me down almost before I had even finished asking the question and I can honestly say was one of the rudest people I have ever met – "Don't even think about it", she said. "She is married and not remotely interested in your colleague. Now kindly leave our stand or I will get you removed". I was a little bit shocked to be fair but I thought it was only fair to go back and tell Percy how it had all panned out. As I may have already mentioned, I had been raised since a child to always tell the truth. "Percy", I said. "I think you are pushing on an open-door mate". He literally freaked on the spot. He couldn't believe I had said something and he wasn't happy. Now ordinarily, if I hadn't been in the grips of this awful condition, I would have listened to my friend and left it there but trade show fever drives you on and takes you to some really dark places, exactly what it did with me that day. Hence why the next bit involves the police.

There were two officers patrolling the exhibition that day and to be fair, much that it was probably an easy shift for them, they looked a little bit bored themselves. In full grip of the fever, I approached them both and asked if they were up for a bit of fun. Happily, they were the exact opposite of Baroness Uptight on the R&A stand and let me know instantly that they were bang up for some mischief and desperate to hear what I had in mind. I shared with them the story of Percy who was still skulking around the stand being all ginger and pissed off and I explained that my approach to the young lady he rather liked hadn't worked out quite as well as we had hoped. And here is where you see the full depravity of trade show fever at its absolute worst. I asked the officers would they be willing to come onto the stand in five minutes time (enough time for me to forewarn every single one of Percy's colleagues) and pretend to arrest him for bothering the young lady on the Royal and Ancient Golf Club stand.

Holy smoke. I don't even recognise myself in these antics but it is one hundred percent true and it should serve as a warning to you all. Before anyone says it and gets all miffed about wasting taxpayer's money on a prank, please don't. I didn't give a monkey about that and rather wonderfully, nor did the police officers. The plan was hatched, I quickly tipped everybody off on the stand and waited for the carnage that ensued. On they walked, looking all tough, in full arrest mode. I had got myself a front row seat stood directly behind Percy and couldn't wait to see how this played out.

"What's your name young man?" they said to Percy. He instantly looked around thinking that they couldn't possibly be here for him. "Who me?" he whimpered as a damp spot appeared on his trousers. "Yes you, we are not asking anybody else are we?". If you have never seen a ginger person with a normally ruddy red complexion go from full red to sheet white in under a second, I can wholeheartedly recommend it. It is hilarious. I was desperately trying to stop myself laughing. These officers had clearly been to acting school or something because judging by Percy's instant crumbling in front of them, he was clearly feeling that he was looking at least a five stretch and he still didn't even know why. "We have received a very serious accusation from the staff at the Royal and Ancient Golf Club about you making threatening and menacing glances at one of their employees". I swear to God, their language was absolutely perfect. I don't really remember the exact words that followed because I was too busy trying to restrain myself and stop the wee coming out. But these absolute gents carried on for another couple of minutes about "accusations, serious consequences, legal processes, damaging outcomes" until eventually Percy turned around and saw me and I literally couldn't hold it in any longer. I was literally dying laughing (sorry, I meant the fever made me laugh, obviously). Percy had had the fright of his life but I decided I should end my fun there just as he teetered on the edge of full cardiac arrest. The whole of our stand erupted and the fever had struck again. When Percy's heartbeat got back below three hundred beats per minute, he turned to me and simply said "You need to remember I work in I.T and I can mess you up really badly". Look, as far as anybody needs to know, it was a dodgy search engine that had taken me to those "adult education" classes. That is my story and I am sticking to it.

So there you go, it links to business travel but like I said, trade show fever warranted a chapter of its own. Be ready for it on your journey towards being less shit. It can get you at any time and strikes without warning. You've been warned.

7.   OBJECTION HANDLING:

One of the things that many people do on their way to becoming a bit less shit is to try and pre-empt some of the problems, obstacles or objections they might run into during the course of a sale. Let's face it, if you are really shit, your daily life is likely to be one major objection and so if you want to get past that, you need to invest at least a degree of thought into the reasons a potential customer might give for not entering into an agreement of sale with you.

To be honest, objection handling was always a feature of every sales meeting I ever attended and it was always the session which everybody thought they got something out of. Think about it. There are all your salespeople in the room at the same time, all of that experience and probably lots of them harbouring the same thoughts and maybe concerns as you are. Your company has just banged the drum, showed you something new to sell and the responsibility of selling it to an insolvent market that is already jammed full of ageing product falls to you! That means the pressure is on and the ability of all of your colleagues to put food on their table rests firmly on your shoulders. You. The shit one. What are your company thinking? Maybe they aren't thinking at all and they are just hoping but for now, your job is to avoid being found out for as long as you can which means you might as well hit up some of the less shit people in the room for the benefit of their experience and work to keep yourself in employment for longer than you probably deserve.

In my experience, we literally used to blurt out on a page, all of the things that a customer might use as an objection to your latest and greatest creation. We would divide into groups and attempt to answer and overcome these objections and then reconvene in a group to share the wisdom with everybody. Now the reality is that some of these objections will be rational and let's just say that others, well, not so much. Going through how to respond to rational objections is time well spent in anybody's book but I wouldn't dwell overly on the irrational or unreasonable. One of the first things you would do well to remember in sales is that there is no point in trying to reason with an unreasonable person. Don't get me wrong, it took me a while to accept this but I am trying to pass on the benefit of my learnings here so that you can be less shit than I was.

It was in fact a favoured saying of my favourite ever boss who always used to tell me "the only person you can't reason with David is the unreasonable person". But when you are young and hungry, you convince yourself that you can sell to anybody and so your boss watches on and allows you to make the same mistakes that they probably did, just like generations that went before and those that will follow on. For me I was in golf when this particular lesson came home to roost. I was enjoying a period of being less shit than a number of my colleagues and I was ravenous for sales numbers. I didn't always stop to think that sometimes you are often better off trying to work your bigger customers for an extra percentage than trying to find new clients, even if my then boss had told me to keep well away from this one client who had dropped onto my radar like a beautiful brand new challenge. I was convinced that I could sell to this particular individual. He was a weird buggar at best but I looked past that and wanted numbers. I know now that I could have saved myself a world of pain if I had listened to my then boss but part of learning is finding out for yourself and so I went to see this chap, blew the doors off and gave him a presentation I was proud of. He would dither, evade my questions but I dug in until he eventually agreed that he needed my product in his life and we completed an order form on the spot. I couldn't get on the phone quickly enough to let my boss know that I had got an order from this person and in fairness to him, he acknowledged my "success" and I felt great. Fast forward several months to this person's delivery and this person's number flashed up on my phone. In my head I was thinking that he was calling to say thanks for the product, it was selling superbly and he would like an early reorder. What he actually said was "I didn't order any of this stuff and you will need to get it picked up ASAP". What the hell? Didn't order it? What a massive unreasonable dickhead. I have done many things in my work life – most of them I am comfortable with, a few occasions where I have underperformed or been unprepared – BUT I have never sent something to somebody that they didn't order. It is sadly fairly common in sales that really shit salespeople do this (it is called the magic pencil) and are too stupid to understand the consequences. But I never did and so when somebody was questioning my integrity like this, I wasn't about to take it lying down. A good reputation in sales is hard earned and quickly lost if dickbags like this individual are stupid enough to fail to remember what they have ordered and that is pretty much what I told him. There was no point in trying to reason with him beyond that and so I didn't. I had learned my lesson. My boss had warned me all about him beforehand but I hadn't listened and the pain I was getting now could have all been avoided. Thankfully, my boss also always stood behind me because he knew me better than I knew myself and so even if this guy called up to complain (erm, I might have said a few things to him in anger), my boss would deal with it and we would all eventually move on. This is the other reason that if you are consistent and work to rules, a person will almost always vouch for you if somebody ever calls your character into question – because they know how you operate. If however you are all over the place, nobody knows if they can vouch for you or not and so they don't. I have had plenty of inconsistent characters on my teams over the years and the quicker you can weed them out, the better. I liken being in a sales group to being in battle and if you are unable to predict whether or not you can rely on your colleagues when bullets start to fly then you are probably better off without them. Fact.

Sometimes an objection can't be overcome and if you have done your best, there is not much point in carrying on with the discussion. I am not talking about burning bridges or being all miffed about it but sometimes you need to recognise when your dialogue is going nowhere. Other times, you are with an unreasonable person (like Mr Dickbag who didn't order his delivery) and again, there is just no point.

Other times, clients may be objecting to you in all sorts of ways and actually there might be a buying signal in among of all of the shit they are coming out with. Sometimes, in order to advance the debate, you just have to tell somebody no. And that's fine. Because very often, the outcome remains the same as it was always going to be – good or bad.

At a similar time to when Mr Dickbag was causing me headaches, I had a major customer in North London and a new person had taken over the buying from her team of professionals who had always been a pleasure to deal with - great lads, Aussies, Kiwis, South Africans – all of them really hard workers and all of them really knew their stuff. Let's just say that she was less enjoyable to deal with – one of those people who wanted everything their own way and lacked the intelligence to realise that if I went "off-piste" for them in terms of what they were asking me to do for them, then I would be likely to do something more for customers that spent more with me than they did. Nobody wins from that game so I operated a level playing field policy which, however hard it can be at times, is without question the best way to run your business over the longer term. In the same spirit of not reasoning with an unreasonable person, I feel very strongly about NEVER being afraid to say no to somebody and so that is often what I did. If you ever doubt yourself on this philosophy, I am happy to share that I said no to this person and within weeks of her filing a complaint about me with my boss and our Managing Director, I had won European Salesperson of the year and been promoted to a managerial post where I would begin to look after members of the U.K team. This was a more dramatic way of proving my point than I would recommend (defending a customer complaint) but I would say that in general, saying no to somebody who is being a bit heavy handed with you very rarely changes the outcome of your negotiation. If you take yourself out of the discussion for a moment, you will see that a person in a position of apparent strength will regularly try to leverage that strength and that is all a part of the great fun of sales. But you don't have to wet your pants at the first sign of this and you certainly don't need to over-indulge anybody who is being a dickbag to you. Sure, it is easy to sit your full weight at any negotiating table when you are representing a market leader or if your product is in huge demand but I have adopted this approach with any of the brands I represented – some of them me-too brands, some of them lacking in real consumer demand, some of them when I really needed the sales numbers (remember, you are never desperate even if you are). But think about it, if you don't respect your own offer enough to sell it professionally, how can you possibly expect a customer to respect you as well? The shitters in the group sold anything to anybody at any price and basically had no rules for how they approached their work. Scatter gun, fling enough shit at the wall and some will stick, doing dodgy deals behind the scenes to grease the slippery pole of success – but none of this works over the longer term. If you are really focused on becoming less shit, you need a plan, an approach, some morals and you need to stick to them. You can work to overcome rational objections but do not over-invest in trying to convince yourself that a dickbag is not a dickbag. And definitely do not be afraid to tell somebody "no" if you feel that what they are asking for is unreasonable or heavy handed.

As a basic practical tip, I used to employ the three strikes rule with potential customers. So, if I went to see somebody about doing business, our offer was not that complex that it required any more than three visits. On the third visit, the potential client would be told to piss or get off the pot (actually, I even used those exact words once to a really frustrating individual). Part of being less shit at selling is the ability to recognise that if you are having to get somebody's arm so far up their back to commit to what you are asking, you are probably already in the wrong place and this resistance will manifest at some future point in the relationship.

8. PROVIDING HIGH LEVEL SERVICE AND HARD WORK

As the saying goes – in order to have what most men don't, you will need to do what most men wont. Insert woman or person if it offends you less but hopefully you get the idea. In fact, I could leave this chapter right there because it is a fairly perfect summation of how this all works.

If I look back and really dissect how I worked in my attempt to become less shit, I have a strong sense that it came from a work ethic that was just in me. Born of industrious parents (who were in turn themselves children of hard-working families), I would be lying if I said that the hard work gene didn't already put me at an advantage. Beyond that, I have been lucky enough to spend a career in sectors that I have been interested in and in roles that have provided a level of challenge. Given those circumstances, I believe that the motivation exists to provide a really high level of service in your daily workplace interactions. For me, it has mainly been in customer facing roles but even before I was trusted to leave work premises and head out to talk to customers, I was already focused on doing a good job (less shit job) for anybody that I came into contact with internally. Now, for the shitters, providing a high level of service sounds like a whole heap of hard work and that might not be what you want to hear. However, take yourself out of the situation for a moment and think about yourself as a customer of anything.

As background, we must acknowledge that if you are planning to be shit in a role that includes service, then if you live in the U.K (where I live), you have chosen an absolutely perfect place to be shit. We don't really expect anything in the way of service, we rarely get anything in the way of service and even when we do, it is so utterly remarkable that we bang on about it to anybody – including strangers - even though the service you are talking about should be the norm!!

On Friday night last week (it doesn't matter month or year, just the fact that it was Friday), I received an email from a really good friend who has been helping me with introductions for a new venture I have become involved in. He had promised me something by Thursday and still hadn't got to it by Friday evening and it was already after 8.00pm. He was mailing me to tell me that he was still working, that his schedule was hectic and that he was just trying to stay focused on outworking everybody else. For him, being less shit could be wrapped up in effort. I responded to him with the opening line from this chapter and then shared with him my own story of completing one of the best deals I ever did at nearly 9.00 on a Friday evening as well. It is amazing to think that as I recounted the story, I could feel the same level of excitement I felt when I was completing that deal in the first place. It resonated at a much deeper level than just "doing my job". I even remember the customer asking me if I was OK to be on the phone talking business at that time of the evening on a Friday. In this particular case it was a driving range and my answer was simple. While he was working selling my equipment, there was no conceivable reason that I couldn't take his call and work for him. This was a really driven individual and his approach back then probably mirrored my own. I have chilled out a bit since then but there is no escaping the truth – there are no shortcuts to any place worth going. It would always crack me up in any environment I have worked in. There would be the people who couldn't get out of their workplace quickly enough as home time came around and there was broadly speaking "the others" who were clearly much more invested in their role than the first lot. Now, I know it is not terribly PC to suggest that one of these ways is better than the other and each of these people had situations and home lives that were unique to them and needed to be considered. However, it was normally the early dart brigade who were the first to come looking for pay rises, the first to bitch and moan if a new vacancy or a promotion didn't go their way or the first to be at the water fountain, ready to slag off their job, their company, their colleagues, their life. Each to their own people, but one thing we are in control of is how we show up on a daily basis including not just for our own job but also our colleagues and those around us.

My contract was a Monday to Friday contract but I have no problem in sharing that I did occasional Saturdays and Sundays for customers who were in real need and where I was able to help them. I am not an advocate of doing this every weekend but I would say that it doesn't take too much for customers to remember you for the things you did that other suppliers wouldn't. It's not rocket science but it is amazing how many people think that something needing to be done is for somebody else to take care of before they put their hand up for it themselves.

In 2014, we were attending the Open Championship at Hoylake on The Wirral. I was chaperoning a U.S colleague for the week. He was a gentleman of the Mormon faith, a good bloke to be fair but he didn't swear, he didn't drink and he had 11 children. I asked him had he ever thought about buying a television. The irony was lost on him but there was probably no point anyway. I mean if you have eleven kids, I can imagine you might be quite tired and probably wouldn't like to stay up late anyway. It is important for you to know at this point that I am partial to the occasional swear word (I contest the old adage that profanity is the refuge of the inarticulate), I enjoy a drink and the Open Championship week tends not to be about going to bed early. In other words, the set up for the week didn't appear to be working in my favour but in my pursuit of greatness (being less shit), I went into that week with the mindset that I would mirror my U.S colleague's actions for as long as I could stand to do so. As I recall, I got through a few days and on the eve of the tournament proper, there were a lot of social gatherings going on and I was finding it increasingly hard to resist. I kept telling myself that I could do this and I stayed sat down in the lounge with my guest while everybody I knew seemed to be rolling in already pissed or heading out to get more pissed. "No, no, no" I kept telling myself and so I figured the best thing I could do was to take myself off to bed.

Ironically, for a chapter on good service levels, we were staying in a customarily shit hotel and within five minutes of going to bed, my colleague knocked on my door to say his steam iron was broken and that he was unable to prepare his clothes for our early start the next morning. He actually rocked up in full Mormon underwear – a sacred symbol of their personal commitment to God which nobody is meant to see. At this stage, all I could think about was my favourite work colleagues who were in stark contrast, demonstrating their own personal commitment to getting shitfaced and which everybody would see. It takes all sorts though right and the U.K is nothing if not diverse? Anyway, I went to bed and fell quickly to sleep until my phone rang at what was probably by then 1.30 in the morning. It was my good friend and colleague and for the purpose of this story, I will call him Lee (because his name is Lee). I have no problem in naming him because he knows I love him dearly. And he is a good worker as well so if telling this story results in him being fired, he will be fine and get another job quite easily I would imagine (mmm, though he is in his late forties now…so maybe not. Ah well, sod it). Anyway, I enquired extremely politely as to the nature of his enquiry "What the flip do you want at this time you absolute shithead" I said. So he told me "We are out and we need a lift. All of the taxis are booked and we need to get to the next party for more drinks. Can you come and get us?"

"Sure, no problem at all mate" I said. "It is not like I am doing anything else at 1.30 in the morning is it you absolute weapon?". And I suppose here is my serious point for the moment. Lee was always very helpful to me and it was a chance (albeit a very inconvenient one hence the abuse) for me to pay him back. I put my clothes on, jumped in the car stone cold sober and went to collect the marauding mob in town. When I got there, another colleague was so drunk he could hardly stand or speak and he was trying to gate crash the lift. I told him to jog on and get a cab because he looked seconds away from being sick and I am very particular about my car. And then a number of other colleagues and customers tried to get in my car. One in the front, four in the back and Lee said he would be fine to get in the boot (trunk). Holy shit. Actually get in the closed in boot of a BMW 5 series, designed to carry home over-priced shopping from Waitrose and expensive golf clubs, not a large gentleman from Nottingham who had drunk his own bodyweight in the old lunatic soup. "No mate" he said. "It's alright, I do this all the time". What? Who on earth does this all of the time and why on earth would you? I kid you not, the car would barely move. My expensive piece of fine German automobile engineering looked more like a Californian lo-rider with the front end that bounces up and down in rap videos. We had to get back to the hotel to lighten the load and I decided I could go back for the dislodged exhaust pipe later on. Lee got out – needless to say filmed by every single mobile phone and looking more like we were people smuggling than helping colleagues in the pissed-up confusion and chaos of the early morning. I went back out to find the very drunk colleague as my conscience got the better of me (and he was a good pal to be fair) but to no avail and I headed back to my bed around 3.30 in the morning. What you then need to know is that my Mormon colleague had insisted on a 6.00 breakfast so that we could get to the course in good time and somehow or another after 150 minutes sleep, I managed to get up and be more or less ready to leave with him on time. Betrayed by my bedraggled appearance, he asked (knowingly I am sure) if I had slept well. I felt obliged to tell the tale. He was a professional man and also a funny man to be fair and rather than the look of disapproval I had half expected, he laughed heartily at my tales of derring-do. I like to think he recognised my willingness to go the extra mile for colleagues and customers that night and was genuinely amused by the mad cap antics.

The point is this, if you want to be less shit, think about what other people do for you – either during work hours like my retail partners who needed my help late on a Friday or on an occasional weekend or people like Lee and our customers who were having a slightly different crisis that night. If you give as good as you get, I genuinely think you will do okay but if you fall on the wrong side of that line, then it will be hard to break out of the competition, either professionally or personally. People I regard as takers in sales (or indeed life) are recognised as such very easily and very quickly. Colleagues recognise you and customers definitely recognise you. This is where these lessons apply well beyond just your career in selling. These are lessons in life.

9. MAKE SURE TO KNOW WHAT YOU ARE DOING / SAYING – DON'T BLAG:

I decided that after the earlier mention of the car-boot dweller Lee, it felt like a good place in the book to mention him again. I love him dearly (I already told you that) and I asked him if he was OK about being name-checked in a global best-seller. Which I think he said he was but I can't really remember so let's just go with it. I was away in the U.S with Lee at the PGA show in Orlando – the world's largest golf exhibition. The point of this chapter is a very simple reminder to make sure that you always know what you are doing (or what you are saying) when you are in a selling situation. For the most part, Lee and I did.

I think the topic of this chapter is very simply borne of one of my own pet peeves, namely somebody attempting to blag me when they are selling to me. I love the process when somebody is doing it well but when somebody is blagging me and clearly doesn't know what the hell they are saying, I get really annoyed. Similarly, I never quite understand most retailer's total failure to train their staff well enough and equip them to sell to members of the public in a coherent manner. I am not talking about expertly but don't take the piss out of somebody by talking absolute bollocks. Especially in the age of the internet. Consumers are informed – even if they are mis-informed, it is still a kind of informed. So it is no surprise that most retailers are shit and that the good ones are few and far between. Think about that yourself for a moment. If you sell to retail, even taking a few moments out to help somebody sell your product is time well-invested. Lazy shitters wont do this though. They think their job is complete as soon as the product is sold to retail but if there is an onward sale to make, it doesn't really matter how much of your product a retailer stocks, it only matters how much of it they sell. I was without question the best in the world (least shit) at product training my retailers. I was not the most knowledgeable – but I was absolutely dialled with the right combination of knowledge and enthusiasm. You might think it cringey now but I used to tell jokes before I did a training session in order to get my audience relaxed and receptive. It removed any sense of intimidation or trepidation about them being there and having to learn and all of a sudden, everybody thrived.

I was aptly reminded myself of the need to know what you are doing on my trip to the Orlando PGA show with my good mate, Lee. We had nipped off for a game of golf this particular day and my friend and I were sharing a buggy. On the opening holes, he was playing like an absolute ninja which was winding me up enormously and with an apparent lack of ability of my own that day, I needed to resort to other tactics to knock him out of his stride. He had left his mobile phone in the buggy each time he got out to play a shot and so I thought I would upset him sufficiently if I reset his phone to a foreign language. I watched him key in his pin code several times and as soon as I thought I had remembered it, I waited for him to jump off the buggy and play his next shot. I grabbed his phone all excited about setting his phone to German and could barely contain myself as I keyed in his PIN. Attempt one failed. Attempt two failed. I had somehow not captured his pin number correctly. He was walking back to the buggy so I went for it a third time and that was incorrect too. Now. What they don't tell you when you buy a certain type of "fruit based" mobile phone is that if you incorrectly enter the pin details three times, the phone wipes itself. Erm, that is not really what I was trying to do. Erm, oh shit. Shit. Shit. Shit. Shhhhiiiiiit!

I had broken my own rule about always knowing what I was doing. He picked up his phone and tried to key in his pin number but clearly nothing was happening. I thought about pleading ignorance for a nano-second, but I am shit at lying and instantly did a brown thing in my pants (he is also known as big Lee) and I confessed on the spot to the crime. As I recall, there is a way to do a reset and get back to a home screen but in the moment, he was livid. He attempted one more shot up the tenth hole, out of sheer fury he smashed it miles down the fairway like a tour pro but was so incensed he threw his club back into his golf bag and stormed off yelling that he couldn't cope with me anymore. Oops. My bad. I skulked back to my hotel room – that is not even a word but, in the circumstances, you will know exactly what skulking looked like and understand how I felt – I was forty years of age and I trudged back to my room like a young kid who had been sent to bed early without pudding. Obviously, there was pudding – I was staying in an expensive hotel and there was as much pudding as you could handle and it was all on expenses, but you get the idea. And then several minutes later there was a knock on the door. It was Lee. The same Lee who had locked himself into the boot of my car in order that others could travel comfortably in the deep leather seats of my fine German automobile. The guy who had been really helpful to me when I joined the organisation where we met. The guy who was in fact helpful to everybody that ever asked him for help – the guy who had now come to tell me that because of my juvenile meddling, his phone had been completely wiped. I thought the reset would be the result he wanted. Sure, he had managed to reset it - but the phone was completely wiped. If I could play sad music to you in a book, this would be an appropriate time because with the phone wiping, gone were some photos of his young twins including a video of one of them saying "daddy" for the first time. I couldn't have felt any worse if I had run the pair of them over (see later chapter for when I actually did this). Lee recalls to this day how my face literally drained as he gave me the news. The moral of the story – know what you are doing or saying in sales and if you want to be less shit than your colleagues, never pretend otherwise. If you don't know what you are doing, educate yourself until you do. The point here is simple. There is absolutely nothing wrong to tell somebody that you are unsure as to the answer of a question rather than looking like an absolute jockstrap and inventing something that is obviously absolute nonsense. Seriously, I have been out with my new venture today and presenting to a group of huge operators just outside Los Angeles and I was as comfortable today to resist a certain line of questioning as I have ever been. I will get back to these guys with the information they require but a sale will not live or die based on information you don't have right that very moment. So don't be pressured into giving bad information or worse still, just making it up as you go along, like I did with Lee's pin code. I gave Lee's phone bad information that day and the outcome was not a good one.

10. ASK FOR THE ORDER

Hey, this is a book about selling. At some point on that sales journey, you might have to ask somebody would they like to place an order. It is utterly remarkable to me that a high percentage of shitters I have worked alongside have been utterly incapable of asking for an order and would clearly much rather stand around drinking coffee and being shit if it meant that they didn't have to ask for the order. There are lots of techniques for helping you with this but ultimately, no getting away from the fact that after your pitch is done and all of the objections are dealt with and your customer is pulling down the roller shutter ready to go home and they have started their car and appear ready to drive off, you might have to ask them for their order. If it helps to reassure you at all, this is OK. No, really. It is OK. I have never known anybody to misinterpret the reason you are stood in front of them rambling on about whatever it is you sell. They don't think for one minute that you have visited just to make them feel good. You have a sales job title, a nice car and a big watch and you would clearly like to sell them something else that they don't need and can't afford. Some of the people I have worked with were much better at this from the moment they drove into an appointment. It was time to get the game face on and the business chat began instantly. Others did their very best to actually talk themselves out of a sale despite being paid in relation to how much they sold. Go figure. I once set up an Inside sales crew with a couple of really great guys, albeit different characters. In the early days, I used to listen to one of them who used to call customers (selling isn't easy over the phone, fact) and he used to say "Are you interested in stocking some of our brand's products or not, no, no, OK then no, thank you, goodbye". And that is before the customer had even had any chance to respond! Now I exaggerate to illustrate here but that is pretty much what he used to do (and I am pleased to say he has gone on to do great things in a different realm which he no doubt accredits to his training with me). So a tip for you in your quest to become less shit. If you get to the point of having done your pitch or you have asked for the order, remember to SUAL - Shut Up And Listen. A customer will regularly tell you what you need to know if you just keep quiet and listen to them as they pour out their thoughts, all of which should inform your next move, whatever that is. I used to see the same thing in retail, not least because some of the guys I called on were hobbyist retailers rather than professional retailers. I remember being at an event when I worked in golf and we used to arrive with all of the kit and give a club's members the chance to trial our latest and greatest. We were working with a female player who clearly had plenty of money and was more than happy with what we had shown her. She wanted to give the club professional her money right there and then and she had believed my pitch that her life would be instantly better if she offloaded a couple of grand on some new kit (which in reality wasn't true because she was absolute shit). But she was loaded. She loved the new kit and she was in a position / the mood to treat herself. Sod it. You can't take it with you right. I pointed her in the direction of the pro and told him that the lady in question would like to offload a couple of grand right now – not least because it would go some way towards helping him pay off the £30 grand or so he owed my brand at that time. And he was like "Sure, we don't have to do it today. Have a think about it. Take your time. We can try a few other options". I was like "For God's sake man, I will take this lady's money in a minute if you don't". It is OK to sell people. If you are doing it right (either selling to retail or selling on as a retailer), it can be to the mutual satisfaction of both parties without any party to the transaction needing to feel bad about what has happened. So, ask for the order, tell your prospect why their life is better with your goods or services in it – don't feel bad about it. Unless you are totally rogue and you really are stitching somebody up.

I said there were techniques for asking for the order or at least working up to the point where you do that. I have seen all sorts of names and acronyms for how best to remember them but they all pretty much boil down to the same thing. This is really, really important if you are serious about being less shit. In a nutshell, start by asking some questions. In the course of giving you their answers, your potential client will give you all sorts of clues as a way of helping you to understand their situation. It is important that they feel you are listening and understanding their requirements and then – and only then – you move in to explain how whatever it is you are selling is the answer to their prayers. It is not difficult. However, 90% plus of people I have worked with have at one time or another (a lot of them always) failed to adhere to this simple structure. Some people call it the last checks before they land the plane. It might be an approach with words you find comfortable (example: if we can do this and you are satisfied about that, am I safe to assume we are going to sign the order?) but whatever it is that gets you there, it is OK to ask for an order.

11. HONESTY

I have touched on honesty already in the book. And it goes hand in glove with dishonesty. So let's deal with it here and move on. I would say that dishonesty has been a consistent hallmark of the shittest people I have worked with and as with dishonesty in any form, you eventually run out of places to hide. I was once attending a sales meeting and we would regularly hear from our marketing colleagues about their various plans and projects which salespeople would then go and share with customers. One of these marketing colleagues was notorious for always being late for meetings. There was a senior sales management gathering one day, we were all sat around our board room table and as usual, this particular character was late. We had received the pre-emptive call from him to say that the M3 motorway was jammed up and that he would be with us as soon as he could. There was enough brain power and sense of mischief in the room to recognize that with a large projector screen in front of us and it being the age of the internet, we could call up a live traffic report in time for our tardy friend's arrival to see if the M3 really was jammed or if he was trying to pull the traffic wool over our road-blocked eyes. Our MD minimized the page on the big screen and was poised and ready for the moment that the lying bastard blundered through the doors sounding off about motorway carnage and catastrophic road conditions. True to form and just moments later, in he walked bitching and moaning about the state of the road but his crack team of shitbag colleagues were already one step ahead. CLICK! Up flashed the live report which showed that the M3 had in fact been clear all morning much to the sheer and absolute horror of the individual in question. Holy shit. To say that we all nearly died laughing at this person's monumental expense would be an enormous understatement, and rightly so. The moral of the story is very clear and is something that my mother instilled in me from a very early age. You can never get in trouble for telling the truth. Sadly this lesson does not seem to have been passed on to certain individuals I have worked alongside. Within a few months this person had left the business. Go figure.

OK. Let's do the honesty bit. In sales, a lot of what relates to honesty links back to what a person says and how they follow through on what they say. Now, I am a pretty honest chap and a very reliable one at that. It might have even been to my detriment but actually, I think honesty and goodness pay themselves back over time. That all said, even this virtuous soul has been occasionally guilty of something short of complete honesty and for me that meant occasionally saying things that I should have just said out loud instead of keeping them in to the point of them coming out in an uncontrolled outburst of frustration.

I ought to have learned this as a youngster from an episode on a school ski trip when I was fourteen. It wouldn't happen now but back then there was a female P.E teacher who used to go on each ski trip and was in fact always nice to everybody and was a good teacher. Let's just say she was very comfortable with herself in a way that most British people aren't and it wasn't unknown for her to mooch about at night in her "nightwear" trying to control young boys like me and my mates while we consistently messed around in our rooms into the early hours. There is absolutely zero suggestion here of any impropriety on the part of the school or the teacher or that we need to revisit Yewtree but the conduct of this particular teacher did give rise to some fairly interesting events. This particular night – and in relation to always being willing to say something to somebody's face – she came into our room and there would have been perhaps five or six of us in there, on bunkbeds and all generally being a pain in the arse. She came in to shut it down in her, ahem…normal bedtime attire, bollocked us and promptly made an about turn as if to leave the room down the little hallway. Except she didn't. And one of my friends didn't notice this. Instead, he was so excited by his first view of a female silhouette, he jumped on the bed, got hold of his "stuff" and duly announced to the rest of us (while he gyrated back and forth) exactly what he would do to the girl's P.E teacher. "Oh yes, I would give it to her good style. She would be getting a large portion" etc, etc and any number of other similar teenage boy's hollow promises. Having heard absolutely everything, the teacher turned back around, came into the main part of our room and looked at my friend who as I recall, still had hold of his, ahem "stuff". "Oh really? Would you really? Is that what you would do?". If you look in the dictionary at the definition of the word "crucified", there is a picture of Jesus alongside a picture of my mate still holding on to his "stuff". The teacher had completely ruined my friend and he was absolutely devastated. As for the rest of us, we were not. We were far from devastated to be fair. We were the very opposite of devastated. In fact, we were laughing so hard I literally thought I might die. The literary world is no doubt grateful that I didn't die that night and my only regret from that episode is that I wasn't smart enough to learn from it.

Fast forward fourteen years and I had demonstrated in my career that I was less shit than one or two others and I had ended up managing a team of sales managers who to be fair (and serious for a moment) were a bit better than your average shit. Except…we had run into a slight issue with one of them and sadly it became irretrievable. As is the norm in these cases, we had to involve lawyers and having narrowly avoided the soul-draining fate of having become one myself, I can't say that where employment lawyers were concerned (with one exception), that they were at that time my favourite flavour. It was a time when as a business we needed real guidance, definitive recommendations and clear insight but we were a wealthy company and it seemed there was more in it for the lawyer if they dragged it out, were vague with their suggestions and instead of simplifying matters, made it as complicated as they possibly could. Bottom line, we were on their clock and they were milking us. Now, I think I might have mentioned I did a qualifying law degree at university (God knows how) and so in that respect, I was no stranger to legal matters and had an ounce of intelligence that enabled me to understand at least the basics. On this particular day, I was working from home and sat at my dining room table while we conference called between myself, my then boss at home in Surrey, our HR leader in Cambridgeshire and our lawyer in

London. Let's just say that as the call went on, I became increasingly confused about the options we had and at one point, I was about to call Stephen Hawkings to see if he could figure it out. But I did then what I wouldn't do today. I simply went along with the call, becoming increasingly frustrated by my lack of understanding and to be fair, pretty bored given that we were at forty-five minutes and counting and I had lost the trail from about five minutes in to the call. These days I would raise my hand, excuse myself for asking a reasonable question and I wouldn't move on until I was clear. This is great advice when it comes to being less shit. If you don't know or something is not clear, ask. Otherwise, how can you be anything else but shit if you don't understand what you are supposed to do. But back then I was different. I was driven by the mantra that it is better to keep my mouth closed and be thought stupid (rather than open it and remove all doubt) – and so I simply said nothing. Eventually, as I left the call for the others to carry on discussing additional business, I said politely that it had been an excellent call and that I was thrilled to now be so clear on our various options. It couldn't have been any further from the truth. I am one of those people where if I don't understand something, I am quickly frustrated and my frustration as we were ending this call was at boiling point. Anyway, I said my farewells and I pressed the button on my phone which would end the call….or so I thought. Still charged up and raging at the fact these imbeciles had probably just had us over to the tune of about five hundred quid and done nothing more than overcomplicate the situation in the process, I had to let my anger go somehow. My girlfriend was in the house with me at the time and I am sad to say that I was in no mood to spare her delicate ears. "Lawyers. F**king, basta*d, shitting lawyers! Lawyers, idiotic f**king stupid lawyers" I yelled at the top of my voice. I know. You are reading this thinking "What an eloquent turn of phrase" but you can have no sense of how angry I was back then. I was absolutely raging. And then, in a flash....terror! Pure, shake you to the core, unadulterated terror. I looked down and noticed that I hadn't in fact pressed the button that would have ended the call and the conference call was in fact still live. "Noooooooooooooooo!!! Shit! Nooooooooooooo. Bollocks! Noooooooooooooo! Flipping buggar etc, etc. Nooooooooooo!!!!". You get the idea. I literally turned sheet white, running up and down the entrance hall in my apartment and for a moment, my girlfriend had no clue what I was doing. She stopped to enquire "What the hell are you doing you madman? What is the matter? You have turned white and you are panicking. What have you done?". I could barely bring myself to speak because in my head I was sure that my outburst was certain to have been heard by the people it was aimed at and the next call I was going to receive was sure to be the same lawyer grinning ear to ear as he administered my own dismissal. I suppose another part of this is owning up when you have done something that is not exactly your best work and I figured in the moment that this was probably my best chance. I was going to man up, give HR a bit more time to end their call with said imbecile lawyers and then I would call them. As it goes, our HR manager was a top lady. Super cool and so in that respect it was an easier call to make than it might have been. With another half an hour past, I picked up the phone and dialled. "Hey Jill. It is David. I owe you a massive apology, what happened there was totally unacceptable and I shouldn't have been venting like I did as a result of my own intellectual shortcomings". "What do you mean" enquired Jill? So I told her about my profane outburst which it turns out she didn't even hear! "Thank God for that I said, you didn't need to hear it either. I was just getting frustrated because I didn't understand it". And then Jill responded. "Oh good", she said. "I am glad you said that. I didn't understand a word of it either".

Moral – if you don't understand, just say so. And turn your phone off. I am now OCD. If I call anybody, I always make sure to turn my phone off at least fifteen times at the end of the call to avoid history repeating itself. How do I know I have finally learned my lesson about just saying something I don't understand? Well, in summer just this year I had an outburst of what I am calling fashion tourettes. I think it was proof that I have actually re-programmed my brain to never feign understanding when something is not clear to me. Now I just say it out loud if something doesn't make sense to me. On this particular day, a young gentleman who worked in the office beneath mine emerged from behind his desk wearing that apparently fashionable combination of dress shoes with three quarter length smart trousers and no socks. As he stood before me, the new hard-wiring took over. "Flip me, what is that!" I said as I pointed at this fashion horror story in front of me. As he looked down all dejected, I was smiling inwardly with the proof I had been seeking for years – namely that I am entirely capable of expressing my failure to understand something and saying it out loud to the person that the situation involves. I might have hurt his feelings but better that than pretending to him or anybody else that I could understand what on earth he was thinking when he got dressed.

12. MANAGEMENT:

I am not sure I've got any funny stories (or at least any I am willing to share) about my management who have had the dubious task of supervising me throughout my career. However, if you have got this far into the book and there is a chance you are going to be less shit as a result of me imparting my various wisdom, then there is a chance you might also fool enough people around you sufficiently and be promoted to a managerial position yourself. But don't worry, you can be a manager and still be shit. Don't start stressing about having to completely abandon your bad habits and actually show up for a proper day's work. With all of this in mind (and if my mind control tricks are working and you are actually starting to believe some of this shit), then I felt there might be a degree of sense in sharing with you some of the things I have enjoyed (and not enjoyed) about my own management along the way. This is a benevolent gesture on my part as I am realistic about the prospect of you working hard enough to actually find this stuff out for yourself. I suppose it depends on your definition of successful management (the least shit) as to how you view the following thoughts. They are only my opinions however they are opinions I respect. Some of the characters I reference here are still in very high-profile jobs so you could argue that the bad things I call out here have not worked against them. It's a moot point but as you know by now, I come at it from a perspective of how they could have been a bit less shit.

Things I didn't like: Here are a few obvious things that I have experienced in various managers and I can more or less guarantee they will not endear you to your troops if you were to copy them yourself.

Megalomania. I have seen this in a couple of characters along the way and it can be frustrating to a megalomaniac's team members. It can regularly manifest as a failure to take into account anybody else's opinion, an overblown inflated opinion of either yourself, your brand, your product, your business or your potential and very often it can be a complete failure to accept prevailing market conditions. These may all sound like the failings and excuses of a shit salesperson but I have enough examples of it over twenty years to sit down and argue with you about it if you want to. In sales (remember, the reason you bought this book), I have seen huge success accompany a manager's ability to empathise, either with an employee or a customer. Megalomaniac's tend not to do so well on the empathy bit. Instead they fix unrealistic goals for the team and play them back to their own management so that everybody inevitably ends up disappointed. You tend to see it in large businesses where everybody is supposed to shit their pants at the prospect of having to "answer to the shareholders". The flip side is when you get to a decent privately owned organisation (I can't recommend these enough) and you work with smart people who truly understand what it is you are trying to achieve such that the work place tends to be a happier place. I have done this more in the later stages of my career and I wonder if the natural vibes of the universe or some other master-minding factors have drawn me to these places by design as I gradually lost all hope for sanity in larger organisations. That aside, if you do end up as a manager in a large organisation, stand your ground for as long as you can about setting realistic goals for your team. The reverse psychology of sales is such that teams who can realistically reach target off the back of a year's worth of hard work are more likely to work harder for you if they feel that what they are attempting is realistic. Equally the converse applies. If you set unrealistic goals and ask somebody to work their bollocks off all year but in the very first month of the year they already know they are chasing an absolute nonsense of a target, it is not rocket science to work out what that does to their morale.

Ego. Everybody has one regardless of whether or not you might like to admit it. However, I have struggled on occasions with managers who have egos which are out of control and put themselves at the epicentre of everything. These characters tend to miss what is going on around them because they are too busy goofing around or giving it the big one trying to impress their own chain of command. If you are going to be less shit in sales management, have a think for a moment about giving your ground troops the kudos of whatever results they are able to generate while you have been sat at your desk fannying about with a spreadsheet. You would be quick enough to jump on them if they are under-performing so surely the converse applies. If they are over-performing, they need to be recognised as such. Sadly, managers with large egos tend to enjoy the credit for things that they mostly didn't do and shirk all of the responsibility when the shit hits the fan. I have seen them prance about as they enjoy work trips and company expense accounts to the absolute maximum while seemingly oblivious to the effect that this can have on your team. Not difficult is it when you think about it?

Things I did like:

Humanity. If you are going to be less shit in life and in management, there is a time as a manager when you need to rely on and trust your own humanity instead of the HR rule book. There will be a time when a team member comes to you with a dog's dinner of a set of problems. In a litigious world, the rulebook will tell you one thing (and there is a place for that) but how you show up as a person in that discussion will be the thing that team members remember you for most. I have a favourite manager in my lifetime and I expect he knows who he is and if I look back at why, it is because he trusted me implicitly, he backed me, he rewarded me and when I needed help, he sure as hell looked after me. My girlfriend and I went through a tough time early on in my career in sales (we were hoping to start a family and I will leave it at that). In the eye of that particular storm, I needed to take a couple of days away from work and my then boss stepped in in the way which summarises perfectly why I have regarded him through life as my second father. And I can't pay anybody a higher compliment than that. He gathered my team members and told them I was out for a couple of days. He told everybody that I was not to be disturbed and then that if anybody had a problem with the arrangements he was making for me, then they were entirely welcome to go and talk to him about it. I don't think anybody went to see him and I expect they could all see what was happening.

Our manager in that moment became the leader and he would have done the same for anybody that worked hard for him. Don't get me wrong, if you were a total shitter, you might not have had the benefit of the same treatment but that is why I have always been a believer in karma. You get out what you put in and it has been proven many times over in my life.

Presence. If you think about it, everybody is generally a part of the machine, trying to get through and generally confronting their own specific set of problems. The other main feature I have enjoyed in my very best managers has been an ability to be present to support me when they could very easily be up to their neck in their own shit. I suppose it links to my point on ego and maybe the guys feathering their own nest because it is all about them are simply too wrapped up in themselves to be present for you. I have knocked around at senior management level for a while and so by definition, I have reported in to MD.s, CEO, Founders, Owners – the whole shooting match. I am pleased to say that there would be at least a couple of them who despite their own mountain of shit they are trying to climb, have always found time to be present for me, enquire about and occupy themselves with my situation and my progress against my goals. It is a finely balanced area this one because I regularly see those without any emotional intelligence bothering somebody senior with nonsense and I think you are lucky enough to not be fired in those circumstances. It is a game of picking your moment and if you are lucky enough to have a manager who is present for you if you navigate that correctly, then you are winning. Kudos too to any manager that is able to pull this off for their team members and not look panicked by the mountain of shit that is normally piling up on their own desk while they sort out everybody else's. It is the price you pay for being less shit than the others and fooling enough other people for long enough to eventually become a manager.

As I write this I begin to wonder if I have been a good manager myself. And do you know what, I reckon I have done alright. Certainly less shit than a few others I have had to work for. If I think about that and why I say I have done alright, it is because in my trusted opinion I have hopefully embodied some of the things I have talked about here. Not ego driven, not a megalomaniac, demonstrating humanity to colleagues and being present for them. If you want to be less shit than your colleagues and perhaps one day climb that slippery pole of success, there are many worse ways to start than by observing these simple traits. One other thing I would add to this is an observation I have made over many years and that is that sometimes leadership involves making difficult decisions and on occasions, it will involve periods of being what reports may regard as unreasonable. I was never really a moaner if my current manager for example didn't live up to the high standards I am talking about here. In fact, I just got on with my job. But the more senior I became in my own career, for whatever reason I saw a belligerence in really senior people that occasionally tipped over into being unreasonable. It is not for here but I have asked myself the question whether or not we all need to be a little bit unreasonable if we are truly going to fulfil our potential. If you want to run a marathon, you might have to sacrifice some family time while you train. Somebody's partner may see that as unreasonable. If you want to climb Everest, you might need to spend more time going up mountains than your schedule will reasonably allow. But once your goals are achieved, the reason returns and normal service is resumed. If your manager is effectively unreasonable all of the time then it may just be that they are a massive tosser and you should think about leaving. ASAFP.

13. LESSONS OF A LIFETIME:

I always told myself that this book would be as long as it was naturally going to be and not ove-extended for the sake of it. In my head, I will make my fortune from the sheer quality of the writing and not how many words I write. Unashamedly, I wanted to make my points and then bugger off back to my yacht that the huge publishing deal paid for. Meanwhile, back on earth, I thought that perhaps the kindest thing I could do for you since you were kind enough to buy this inane drivel, would be to include a very short summary of lessons learned over my lifetime in sales which I could talk about for hours. That said and if I did, you would get bored and the diminishing returns you get from my rambling would prevent you buying any of the next seven editions of this nonsense I already have lined up. Equally, I realise that for average shitters, you have done quite well to get to this point in any book and have demonstrated enough commitment to being less shit and maybe even surprised yourself. You have read my stories and the morals thereof from a life in sales, my views on management and to finish off, here are some more general sales principles that may just help you to finally conquer the mountain that is your eternal quest to be less shit.

KEEP THE FAITH:

At some point in any sales business, your faith in what you are doing will be tested to breaking point and, in some cases, beyond. People (in life generally, not just sales) love to tell you your fortune but I am not quite sure how they know the end to the story that YOU have not yet written. It is not up to anybody else how your story ends and so don't let it be. From a selling perspective, unless you are selling something completely nonsensical, you will have something to sell that is either a quality proposition, a price proposition, a fashion proposition or a need proposition. And probably all sorts of other propositions. But the point is this, as long as you are clear enough to convey to your customer the proposition and the place that what you sell has in the market, then you will sell something if you have faith in what you are doing. I have worked for all sorts of brands in lots of different sectors and I have learned new skills in every single one of those environments. Don't get me wrong, if you sell cars, it might be nicer to sell a Bentley than a Vauxhall Corsa but each product has a market and you will learn something valuable from time spent in either environment.

TALK ABOUT BENEFITS:

This one may seem a little obvious but believe me, in practice I see more people miss this out than the other way around. If I consider why this might be, I have worked mainly in what I call "enthusiast" sectors and sold things that people tend to get excited about. People who sell "enthusiast" products tend to bang on about this feature and that feature and this colour and that colour and this gizmo and that gizmo and they very regularly overlook the reason why the person they are "speaking at" should give a shit. It is in fact staggering how many salespeople set off down this road only to find it is typically a sales dead-end. I will buy something from you if it solves a problem I have, if it brings cost-efficiency or time efficiency or guarantees to make me look like David Beckham with an exact replica of his bank account. To be honest, that is all that most people being sold to care about. Why should I care? Why, why, why? Start With Why – one of my all-time favourite books. Not what or how but why.

I used to run a brand in Europe that had amazing technology at its disposal but it didn't have the rock-star credibility of its bigger sister brand. This meant that we had to find a way of selling it up against much louder, higher profile and to be fair, straight-up sexier competition. Thought about logically, the benefits of selling a product that every single other retailer stocks can be many. In this instance, I used a reverse psychology position to sell my lower-profile brand which I liken to "sell by not selling". Customers I had known from my days at higher profile brands would come and see me and enquire about this new brand. I would always be super low-key about it and happily open up with "yes, it is great product but probably not for everybody Bill". Bill would sometimes enquire further as to what I meant and so I went on. "It depends on what you want to sell Bill. If you want a ready-made queue of customers outside your shop door demanding a product by name, then this probably isn't the one for you. People know it but maybe not as much as some of those Rockstar brands you stock". There is a hidden benefit in this comment that would be obvious to anybody familiar with the sector. The products that everybody stocks and everybody wants tend to end up driven down on price to the point that a retailer makes no profit from them. But the retailer feels good because they are selling something. So what I am actually saying to the person in this instance (albeit suggestively), is that "there is half a chance you can make some money from selling a lower profile product". Mmm. Now that sounds like a benefit where I come from. I would carry on. "This line tends to work best if you are into supervised product trial Bill. We know the technology works and so if you are hell bent on getting the right thing for an open-minded consumer, then this product certainly stacks up from a facts and figures perspective". What I am really saying here knowingly is that everybody in the sector at the time wanted to be into supervised product trial, sell equipment that was bespoke manufactured for the consumer and move away from stocking masses of generic product that everybody else stocked. If Bill was doing his homework on this, he was already starting to think that my brand was going to enable him to carry a lower stock level and simply buy products from me on a made to order basis. That sounds like benefit number two. You get the idea. While I was established enough in my field and experienced enough to manage these conversations, I was always all about helping my customers to see the benefits of my brand and thinking about doing things differently (if that is what was required). Sure, you don't win them all but we all like and identify with benefits. The only reasonable conclusion I can therefore draw if you fail to mention these benefits in your sales pitch is that you are an absolute sales shitter. Listen up. Be less shit.

YES BEFORE PRODUCT:

This links nicely to the above point (benefits) and is one of the most recommendable philosophies I could share with anybody. Once again, no graphs and charts to prove it but

I would say that your odds of securing a sale with this approach are manifold the odds if you go hard on a features download and simply bombard your customer with a machine gun rendition of the latest and greatest. Yes before product is a very simple technique where you start with the why of your proposition (including the benefits) and if you are selling an actual physical product, you hold-off from showing it until the real emotive, benefits, why they should give a shit conversation has been finalized. At my absolute best (which is still not very good), I would have virtually secured a sale before I had even showed my product. In fact I would go as far as to say that it was largely irrelevant what I would have shown afterwards if I had handled that front part of my presentation correctly. Yes before product. This is the absolute shizzle if you can get your head around it (whatever that means). You find a state where your customer is buying into much more than a product. They are buying into you. Your manner. Your professionalism. Your sense of trustworthiness. They are going through that 75% of the decision built on more subjective foundations before they finally ask you "Hey, I better see this thing I just spent twenty-five grand on". This is the 25% objective justification of their subjective decision and unless your offer is absolutely bereft, your deal is unlikely to fall over if you can get it to this point. In fact, if you can master this, you are definitely less shit than some of your colleagues.

I would probably add here that some of this depends on your personality type – I tend to be excitable and was known for enthusiasm. If I had paid you a sales visit, I am not saying I took the doors off your shop but you would have known I had been. Again, don't get me wrong. I don't want to turn the process into a circus. Of course, you must be able to back up all of the excitement with a rational presentation of the "need to know" stuff but be very careful not to bore people. People act on emotion and if they are already bought in emotionally to the sale, a too long presentation of the facts and logic may actually start helping to talk them out of their decision.

SIMPLICITY AND MOMENTUM:

I can't actually believe how much good stuff I am passing on in this book already (given that I foresee being able to write and sell at least another several iterations). One of the best things I can tell you is that simplicity in selling will be your best friend. Simplicity creates momentum and momentum creates sales. That is the big heading and I would just say that you should think about how you can inject simplicity into your approach to sales. It might be a summarised communication (rich coming from me because I was regularly linguistically indulgent) or whatever else – just make sure that good simple communication is a feature of every approach. If I reflect on when my life in sales began, there was not as many distractions for people, not as many social-media based demands on a person's time, not as many agendas, not as much noise. Maybe that helped me to be as focused and as simple in my approach as I was back then and if I am honest, I haven't felt anywhere near as focused since. That is a massive acknowledgement I have only just realized that I made. I was in my target. I was on my target. I lived and breathed my target. In fact, if I look back to my biggest and best customers over a lifetime in selling, the transactions with every single one of them – without exception – were the simplest. If I think about the times I came away from a call the most excited about a meeting I had just been a part of, it would have normally been with a big customer who understood and respected my approach, wasn't interested in dicking me or my brand around and understood that there was a way to complete a transaction to the mutual satisfaction of both parties. Sometimes, the simplest transactions were the result of absolute trust and that is a happy place to get to if you are selling. I will say it again. Simplicity brings momentum. Momentum brings sales. One of my all-time favourite customers was a part-owner of a golf course, property developer, wheeler-dealer and all round great human being. He knew he was going to be looked after and as such he had total trust in any of the transactions we did together. Sometimes, he just wanted to support the sales guys he liked but this was never a concern because everybody did everything they could to pay back his support and then some. It was always simple. No reason it shouldn't be that way every time. It wont be. But it could be.

PERSPECTIVE:

One message I would like to convey is that however into what you are doing you are, selling is very rarely a matter of life and death. Good selling requires a sense of perspective and a balance such that you don't "overegg the pudding". I was into what I did but I never let it get the better of me. You are never desperate even if you are. If I think back to stressing a bit and freaking trying to get ready for meetings, I believe I could have performed better by not being drawn into the nonsense. If I could have worked past my imposter syndrome, brought my offer to the table with absolute conviction and been more prepared to call bullshit where I saw it, maybe my path to here would have been different but I have recognised those things and on the basis that it is never too late to learn, they remain things I can still apply to this day. My other watch out under this heading is to also not come over as being consumed in your role on social media. I have observed this for a while and I have no problem posting work-related content or sharing content on my own channels within reason. But I look at former colleagues' activity on social these days and it can sometimes look as though they have been brainwashed. Behind anything you sell there is YOU the person and YOU will be a major part of anything somebody chooses to buy from you. There is a difference between being into something and being consumed by something and it is this sense of perspective and measure that can certainly help you on a daily basis.

WHAT HAPPENS NEXT:

To manage expectations, I am good but I can't profess to know what happens next. The workplace is finely balanced in lots of different ways and tomorrow is promised to nobody. Large corporates get larger, I have no sense of how hard people are working (now versus the past) but as an observer from a slight distance over the past couple of years, I would be honest and say that the prospect of ever having to work once again in a large corporate doesn't really excite me. Sure enough, I would do it if I had to but I have had a sort of awakening in my time away from the conventional workplace and seen for myself (and been around) people who make a living in all sorts of different ways. There is something about the entrepreneurial path that has drawn me more of late and I think it has been this curiosity which has drawn me to my current role in an exciting technology start-up business that will still initially focus on sport. I only share this as a means of encouragement to anybody who feels that a role in a large corporate might not be for them and to remind them that there are other opportunities out there today that might not have even existed even just a year ago. Nobody needs to feel condemned to a lifetime of doing something that doesn't really float their boat. While I have said several times already that I have few regrets, I have wondered about the outcome if I had started in an entrepreneurial environment earlier. It is all ifs, buts and maybes really but at least I have got to see there are lots of different and exciting things you can do with your sales experience and I have acted on that. That I have chosen to undertake this latest venture with some very smart people will hopefully also serve as a recommendation to anybody reading this to do the same thing.

ONE LAST NUGGET:

I was thinking about how to sign off a book about being less shit and after going round and round with ideas of all kinds, I come back to something that I find myself regularly referencing as a benchmark in the workplace. It is frank and some will no doubt say it is outdated but I couldn't care less to be honest. My benchmark is this – if you were in a conflict situation and about to climb out of your trench with your colleagues and do what was known in war time as "going over the top", ask yourself who you would want to have alongside you. My view is that with the right people, I wouldn't even need to look left and right to know if my colleagues were coming with me. In the right team of people, you should be able to say without hesitation that your colleagues are coming with you, no questions asked. In the spirit in which we started this book, it is a fair assumption that the absolute shitters wouldn't make the team for a mission like this. And if we accept that we can't all be the best or highly effective, at least try to be less shit than you are today and either make sure you are on the team or be somebody that others would want for their team.

Finally, I hope that in among the silly stories, you have picked the sense out of pointers and advice that are intended to be within the grasp of anybody who can be remotely arsed enough to turn up and actually earn their salary. In fact, I would go as far to say that it you are in sales today and put into play some of the learnings I have shared in this book, I genuinely guarantee you will be less shit at sales tomorrow. I would even be happy if you simply felt better for hearing some of my own experiences and have identified reassuring similarities with experiences of your own. In some way, shape or form, we really are all just trying to get through. If we can be a bit less shit, have some fun and and help each other along the way, that might be a really good place for us all to start. And finish.

Printed in Great Britain
by Amazon